"When conflict threatens your marriage, don't run from it—pick up this book instead! Through this biblical and practical guide, conflict becomes a pathway to deeper intimacy. Here's scriptural, insightful, and tested advice you can put into practice right away—with results that could save and sweeten your relationship!"

Lee Strobel
Author, *The Case for Christ*
Professor of Christian Thought
Houston Baptist University

"Take It to the Cross is THE book I recommend to everyone who is experiencing conflict in an important relationship. The principles in Dr. Paul Looney's book have changed the lives, marriages, and families of hundreds of people in our church because they are centered in the life changing power of the cross of Christ."

Kerry Shook
Co-founding pastor of Woodlands Church
Co-author of NY Times bestseller -
One Month to Live

"This conflict resolution tool has saved and enriched thousands of marriages. It is a simple relationship tool that a child can remember and powerful enough for tough mature issues. It is dynamically structured to appeal to our spiritual commitment while allowing voice to our hearts, minds, and intent to help us grow as married couples. My wife and I have led thousands to use *Take It to the Cross* and consistently hear of its success."

Stew Grant, D.Min.
Center for Healthy Relationships

TAKE IT
TO THE
CROSS

For Couples

From Conflict to Connection

Paul A. Looney, MD

Published by: Thrown Pot Press

Take It to the Cross
Copyright © 2016 Paul Looney

Inquiries may be addressed to
Dr. Paul A. Looney
26205 Oak Ridge Dr, Suite 106
The Woodlands, TX 77380

ISBN-10: 0692642129
ISBN-13: 978-0692642122

Author's Website: PaulLooneymd.com
Email address: PaulLooney@gmail.com

DEDICATION

For Teri, my one perfect rose. I love you!

TABLE OF CONTENTS

PREFACE

My wife, Teri, and I have been leading couples retreats since the early 1990's. She has been my mainstay in all that led to this book and the tool it conveys.

Our dear friends, Dan and Linda Wilson, are also a huge source of support. Years ago, they invited us to join them in New Orleans for a marriage weekend sponsored by Christian Medical Dental Society. Subsequently, we became a part of the CMDS council on marriage and met Chuck and Sandy Crown from Denver. Like me, Chuck was a psychiatrist, and Sandy a therapist. Influenced by the work of Sherod Miller, Chuck and Sandy showed us how to take turns standing to reveal thoughts, feelings, and proposals around an issue. Over time, practicing these concepts led to the development of *Take It to the Cross*.

I owe a debt of gratitude to our ministry supporters and all who attended our workshops and retreats. With them, and the support of Hidden Manna Ministries' board, the tool has been honed and become increasingly effective. Thank you Jerry Brooks, Dan Wilson, Stu and Suzanne Taylor!

Joanne Hillman got the book started by transcribing and editing many hours of "One Flesh" retreat recordings and Stew Grant gave me a strong push to publish the tool in book form. In addition to all the work Teri put into the manuscript, Shivana Khosa and Emily Ballard did extensive editing as well. They, along with Suzanne Taylor, made suggestions and contributed

1

their writing to make this a better book. I have also received tons of support and encouragement from Pat Guth and all our lay counselors at Woodlands Church. In particular, Jeff and Kelly Ward have further shaped the use of this tool in their extraordinary work with hurting couples. And a huge thank you to Maria Grace for her invaluable guidance in the publishing process, cover design, editing, formatting, and for pushing me along through the narrow passage of finishing this book.

I am also deeply in debt to Kerry Shook, my senior pastor at Woodlands Church, and to Randy Reeves, our executive pastor. Working with them has been a huge blessing in equipping me for ministry.

Over the past twenty years, Teri and I have refined and taught *Take It to the Cross* to thousands of couples. The stories in this book are our story and theirs. I hope you will recognize your story here as well. Except for my own marriage, names and details were changed to disguise the identities of actual persons involved.

We all struggle to be authentic and open when it comes to sensitive issues, and we yearn for wholehearted engagement with those we love. But we all need help negotiating the challenges of communication and oneness, and marital intimacy goes far beyond the bedroom. It has to do with being known. We all want to connect emotionally, spiritually, and intellectually, as well as connecting physically. When we share from the heart we offer an invitation to intimacy—"into me see." And ironically, we can only fully know ourselves in an attuned relationship where we give and receive truthful and loving feedback.

In addition to its usefulness in marriage, *Take It to the Cross* has been applied with great success for negotiating and problem solving in the workplace, in churches, and in schools. It works by helping participants set aside defensive impulses so they can enter in with openness, honesty, and respect. It promotes courage, inviting each one to tell the truth when it would be easier to conceal feelings and needs. It provides focus and helps participants stay on topic. It supplies structure and concrete assistance so we can hear and be heard.

Truth and love are essential for all our relationships, but one without the other spells disaster. While some of us take pride in being honest, we may err on the side of brutal honesty. Others of us don't ever want to seem unloving, so we compromise the truth by sugar-coating or withholding our deep feelings and desires.

In Ephesians 4, the apostle Paul teaches that speaking truth in love is a key to spiritual growth and maturity. For if we are not anchored by deeply held values and beliefs, we will likely waver back and forth in response to others' agendas. In contrast, when we learn to take a stand for ourselves, declaring who we are, what we believe, and what we need, we can grow along with others in a healthy way.

"Instead, speaking the truth in love, we will grow to become in every respect the mature body of him who is the head, that is, Christ. From him the whole body, joined and held together by every supporting ligament, grows and builds itself up in love, as each part does its work." (Ephesians 4:14-16)

So while we don't want to be infantile, being childlike can help us grow. Children are open, accepting, curious and loving and they grow through trusting relationships. Healthy marriages grow us up, allowing husband and wife to engage full and freely as children of God. The safety of marriage supports vulnerability and healthy couples commit to a relationship offering lifelong companionship and mutual support.

If we avoid struggles, we decline the invitation to mature. Engaging them takes energy, to be sure. But avoiding conflict or difficult topics drains the union, taking more energy from us than we can possibly imagine.

Yes, addressing conflict is work. It exposes weaknesses, fears, and shortcomings—all parts of our human condition. But it is good work, because learning to address difficulties and differences with love and truth brings connection and growth.

CONFLICT! WHO NEEDS IT?

Jesus didn't want the cross. Even down to the last hour, He asked for another way. "My Father, if it is possible, may this cup be taken from me" (Matthew 26:39). Even so, He was willing. If it was the only way to accomplish what His Father God had in mind, He would go there.

Conflict can be like that for us. It is often the last thing we wish to face, especially with those we love most. Yet at times, tough conversations are pivotal in moving our relationships to the next level, stimulating maturity and intimacy. Like the cross of Jesus, engaging necessary conflict is God's way, and we must be willing to walk through it with His help and direction.

Of course, we need to know outcome will be worth the discomfort. Our brains are wired to spur us on toward pleasure and to shun all pain, so we need a compelling reward to override the natural tendency to resist the burn of conflict. Jesus had such assurance when He went to Golgotha. Hebrews 12:2 affirms, *"For the joy set before him he endured the cross, scorning its shame."* Jesus was positive His Father would honor obedience and make it worth His while. We must believe that, too.

As a matter of fact, there is a colossal payoff. Couples who learn to navigate conflict well are more likely to stay the course.

They bond in the trenches of adversity and they find solutions to problems that over the course of time would cause much more misery than addressing them head-on as they arise.

So while conflict is stressful, stress is part of life. Teri and I cannot do life together without running into obstacles, and my way of dealing with them doesn't always jive with her idea of a good plan. We often disagree. And this is by our Maker's design. Points of friction are inevitable when we marry someone of the other sex— one who is a unique blend of personality, character, and needs. God made us different and gave us the desire to couple. And we are biologically predisposed to choose someone who complements us immunologically as well and temperamentally.

As it turns out, stress can actually have a positive impact on us as long as we welcome it as a normal part of living. In her TED talk, "How to Make Stress Your Friend," Kelly McGonigal shares how viewing stress as a bad thing is actually what makes us more susceptible to its ravages. To resist it, primes us for heart attack or stroke. If we embrace it, though, it can actually help us thrive and experience joy. In the talk, Ms. McGonigal shares how reaching out and connecting in the face of stress forges strong bonds.

In a similar fashion, it is our resistance to conflict that takes the biggest toll to our souls, our bodies, and our relationships. Jesus' brother, James, urges us to *consider it pure joy* when we face various trials (James 1:2). This most certainly includes the trial of facing the abysmal gaps between the needs and desires of husband and wife, whether in finances, sex, parenting, work, or fulfillment.

You Can't Escape!

Conflict happens. When two or more people engage in a committed endeavor, they will encounter disparity in personality, purpose, and priorities. If these are not addressed, the partnership may fail or the project be abandoned. This is especially true of marriage, where stakes are high and exit doors barred. If we want a deep connection, we must learn to stay in the room and engage conversation to move from power struggle to peace.

This book can help you. But it will hurt you, too. It requires an unswerving commitment to engage directly and lovingly, even when every cell of your body is telling you to attack, defend, or run away. It hurts to die to self-protective urges, but that is exactly what is required to span the gap between two hearts in conflict.

The communication tool described in this book won't work for everyone. Some people absolutely refuse to try it, saying it seems contrived or goofy. It makes them feel awkward or exposed, and they are right. But with a willing attempt, I have seen it generate almost miraculous results.

What stands in the way is almost always pride or fear. We don't want to feel or appear vulnerable, unsure, or weak. Nor do we wish misunderstanding, judgment, or rejection. We would remain fortified by self-protection, feeling somehow sheltered and snug in a familiar, dark gloom.

Some won't try *Take It to the Cross* because we don't want to feel the pain of disappointment or failure, and we don't want to give our partner a chance to hurt us again. As children we may have vowed never to feel a certain brand of pain ever again and we will be damned rather than be forced back into that wound. We loathe feeling small again and spurn any invitation to loosen our grip on the steering wheel. Looking good, feeling good, being right, and being in control can serve as idols, blocking the way to love.

Unfortunately and gratefully, Jesus calls us out of comfort to the cross. *"Then he said to them all: 'Whoever wants to be my disciple must deny themselves and take up their cross daily and follow me'"* (Luke 9:23).

Not all pain is created equal. Sharing deep desires, hurts and needs from a heart of love is good pain even if it does not give the hoped-for result. From this vantage point, the pain of the cross was profoundly good even before it produced the desired result, because the cross was the definitive expression of God's love.

In the cross God revealed His heart for us, but not everyone chooses to view it with love and compassion. Not everyone is interested in seeing God or connecting with Him, particularly when He shows up in an unattractive or inconvenient way. Many of us are so committed to avoiding pain that we don't even want to have it in our field of vision.

The apostle Paul says that the message of the cross is foolishness to some, but power to others (1 Corinthians 1:18). When we walk the *Cross* described in this book we may feel foolish and weak. But God uses it to release grace to us and through us. When we share that we feel foolish and weak, our partner is invited to be wise and strong for us. And when they expose their tender spots, we can respond with gentle grace. We all need someone to love us at our worst and hold us at our weakest.

The risk of vulnerability is scary stuff, but it makes us more alive. Like walking out on the high wire, pressing through terror leads to exhilaration. In contrast, playing it safe does not produce a searing pain, but rather a numbing ache, and persistent avoidance of addressing it can kill. Each time we back away from authentic communication, we die to the possibility of secure attachment.

If we ask Him, God will be our safety net when we step out and fall, but if we refuse to trust enough to push through avoidance and risk enough to connect through conflict, we will find ourselves missing out on love.

The best resolution to a clash of wills is always based on understanding and love. If we share only our strength and our logic, we will end up with solutions that may be "right," while at the same time being entirely wrong. This tool will help you be lovers, not lawyers.

Take It to the Cross will help you bravely explore the wilds of your life together. As you go there, you will discover that genuine disclosure is in many ways its own reward. You will feel better, more peaceful and more joyful as you become fearless in your most significant relationships. Being authentic is deeply satisfying.

Don't forget that God is for you. He is the author of peace, and marriage is His idea. But remember, too, there is an enemy. Satan is fully committed to destroying what your Heavenly Father plans to build. If you don't speak up in your marriage and other important relationships, the enemy will happily fill in blanks in the conversation. He is masterful at undermining trust and fostering suspicion about the quality of our loved one's commitment to us.

So go there! Engage those troublesome topics. Intimacy is worth it. The fresh vistas that open up after slogging through a dark valley of strife to that next steep peak are breathtaking. And the creative possibilities that arise when we trust God enough to set aside judgment and fear are astounding. We simply must give everything to the adventure.

You Need Help!

When it comes to sensitive issues, we all need help. Finances, parenting, and sexuality, to name a few, can set off our defenses and insecurities dramatically. If we are not careful, our strong reactions will leave us feeling we are on opposite sides of the issue. The truth is, both partners usually want good things for the relationship, but neither knows how to approach these problems without causing harm.

And while often appearing as a barrier to intimacy, conflict also provides an invitation for deep connection. This, I believe, is God's design. He causes romantic love to flourish in the presence of differences in our bodies and brains, so it makes sense we will be attracted to someone who addresses life in a way vastly different from our own. So the very places we struggle present the next frontier for exploration in our union. Like the differences of our sexual anatomy, relational differences allow us to come together in a beautiful way when we honor one another and learn how to move together in the face of those differences.

The path to intimacy can be thrilling and terrifying. Sometimes it is delightful—like a walk in the park. At other times, it is like trying to cross the freeway on foot during rush hour. How do you get to the other side without getting run over or causing a wreck? We all need a path through conflict that is safe and direct—a path to move us further along our relational journey. *Take It to the Cross* is like a crosswalk, moving us from danger to safety, from pain to peace.

Conflict and Affairs

I recently attended a workshop on infidelity with John and Julie Gottman. They are at the forefront of marriage research, so I listen when they speak. I was struck by their assertion that whenever there is an affair, there is conflict avoidance. As I thought about my own experiences counseling couples, I came to believe the Gottmans are right. And if they are, learning a healthy way to address conflict may be one of the best ways to make your marriage safe from affairs.

When a couple decides to marry, their relationship is sealed with vows. Each one promises to be faithful, to cherish, honor, and protect one another. The walls guarding marriage stand on these vows. Early on, our resolve and energy are at an all-time high. However, as days go by, we tend to get lazy and distracted from the centrality of our union.

Realities of life such as jobs, schedules, household chores, and financial obligations sap energy and limit our face-to-face time, often leaving both partners feeling neglected and disconnected. Pregnancy and childbirth often cause a huge dip in marital satisfaction. If a couple does not have effective methods for addressing their concerns, issues pile up and obstruct intimate contact. Over time, more unsolved problems accumulate, and the barrier grows.

Eventually, our longing for connection leaves us susceptible to fantasies of a better life with someone else. If we are not careful, it becomes easier and easier to look for an ally outside the marriage rather than attempt the formidable task of dismantling the wall that has produced our sense of alienation. Unsuccessful attempts to address difficulties can breed even more discontent and discouragement. We may end up feeling hopelessly disconnected.

If faithfulness is not reinforced, or if one partner or the other has experienced a breach in healthy boundaries through sexual or emotional violation in the past, the risk of infidelity grows. Even a family history of infidelity or divorce may damage the integrity of the boundary protecting the marriage. If this wall erodes, peering over it becomes ever more likely, allowing a "greener grass" view—the illusive dream of a relationship free of misunderstanding or disregard. In some cases, it is only a matter of time before the conflict-avoidant couple finds one or the other reaching for outside offers of intimacy and fulfillment.

Is 'Take It to the Cross' for All Problems?

You may be wondering if there are certain conflicts *Take It to the Cross* is not equipped to navigate. While I have seen the tool work wonders for couples with a wide gamut of problems, it does have limitations. For especially traumatic experiences such as physical abuse, addiction, or infidelity, I suggest seeking guidance of a pastor or counselor to help you and your partner through the issue. Even so, *Take It to the Cross* can help you navigate through some of the choppiest waters.

Conflict is not optional. Thankfully, though, there are options in how we deal with it. The keys are planning and patience. Bolting across a busy street on impulse could land you in the morgue. Waiting for the proper signal at a crosswalk can be frustrating, but it is safer for you and for others. Some of us lack the willingness to step into conflict, while others lack the patience to wait for the right time. Learn to engage *Take It to the Cross* and you will be amazed at the new avenues that open for you and your mate—spiritually, sexually, emotionally, and intellectually.

The Fun of Friction?

Yes, friction in a marriage can certainly rub us the wrong way. But while friction between folks is often seen as a bad thing, think about sexual intimacy. Mutual satisfaction in this most intimate of acts uses friction to good advantage—learning to rub one another the right way. To do this, our approach must be considerate and well-timed, honoring the sacredness of sex and our mate. We must also be good at reading our partner's cues in order to maximize pleasure and to back off when there is discomfort or fatigue.

There are many reasons people avoid sex, but not because it's bad. Fear and pride are probably the big ones. We don't want to feel embarrassed and we don't want to be hurt. We fear vulnerability. Sharing ourselves physically and emotionally— being honest about our fears and fantasies— is risky business, but the payoff can be huge. We connect and life can result!

Engaging conflict challenges us in much the same way as sexual interaction. We back away from it because we are afraid of being hurt or being made to feel small or inadequate. But we can all learn to be like Jesus. He came as a baby, small and inadequate, naked and helpless, in order to communicate God's love to us in a tangible way. And He died in the same way He came—naked and helpless. But God honored Jesus' commitment and vulnerability. Through the cross, our Father made a way to connect with all of us despite our weakness and fear.

Take It to the Cross will allow you to be more like Jesus and to honor God and your partner in your difficult conversations. You will find it easier to be open and vulnerable so that you bring all you are to the discussion. You might even think of the tool as a good lubricant to reduce the friction in your conflicts, because friction can hurt us or it can be pleasantly stimulating. So can conflict, depending on how we manage it. If we approach it from a win-win point of view, we can learn to be gentle, but deliberate.

You may think conflict should not be difficult and a good connection should come without effort. But what comes naturally for most of us when we feel threatened or disregarded is to withdraw or become defensive. We demand or manipulate, we argue or nag. All of these natural maneuvers are likely to undermine the partnership, even if we get what we want. We need a way to override or short-circuit our normal reactions to conflict. The design of this tool will help.

Sex is most satisfying when both partners are fully engaged. Resolving conflict is the same. *Take It to the Cross* will help you achieve this harmony. Being "all in" for your difficult conversations will smooth the path for your other, deepest connections.

Conflict, like sex, can be messy; becoming one is worth it!

A QUICK PREVIEW

In a nutshell, *Take It to the Cross* gives us confidence to approach conflict from a peaceful place. Its structure helps avoid destructive patterns that derail tough conversations.

Either partner can bring up an issue and the two together set a specific time and place to meet for up to thirty minutes without interruption. Face-to-face is preferred, but the tool also works by phone or video conferencing. If together, the one going first stands at the head of the cross while the other sits at the foot of the cross without speaking.

Sticking to one topic at a time, the first partner begins by defining the issue, then revealing "What I Wish," "How I Feel," and "What I Think." After fully relating desires, thoughts, feelings and fears, the speaker makes a proposal--a concrete action intended to bring harmony and cooperation. Finally, a statement of "Where I Stand" anchors the conversation in love and faithfulness. The seated partner is encouraged to take notes.

Then roles are reversed and the second partner takes the floor, while the other sits at the foot of the cross. After a brief restatement of what has been heard, the second partner walks through the same process.

Visually, *Take It to the Cross* looks like this:

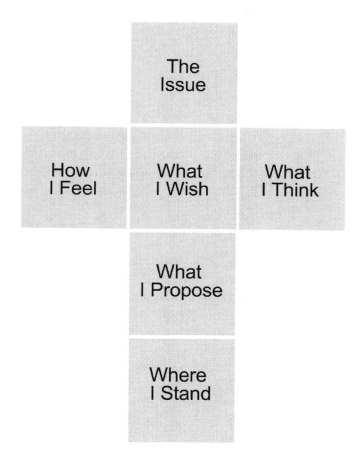

TAKE IT TO THE CROSS

The
Issue

How
I Feel

What
I Wish

What
I Think

What
I Propose

Where
I Stand

Several rounds may be necessary to reach agreement, but this tool facilitates amazing results. Not only will you find relief from tension and conflict, you will feel closer to your mate. Like anything, though, growth comes with practice. Even if you still digress to hostility and demeaning words while attempting to *Take It to the Cross*, don't despair. Repeated effort and a little coaching and prayer will help you learn to do business with kindness and respect.

CHAPTER ONE

GO THERE! CONFLICT AND INTIMACY

"Don't even go there!" Jessica said.

She and Brad were both tired. It had been a long week, and they were getting ready for bed. Brad had just inquired about the water bill.

"What?!" Brad frowned, put off by her response. "I just asked a simple question!"

"Right!" she glared, "And why is it always my responsibility to pay the bills? You can do it as easily as I can."

"Fine, then. Forget I asked! I guess I'll just assume I can't count on you for anything!"

So begins a weekend for Jessica and Brad. Without some repair to the relationship, the weekend promises to be rocky.

Sadly, both partners had good intentions, but they failed to communicate desires and needs effectively. In a matter of moments, they went from fine to feuding.

The truth is, Jessica felt bad that she had failed to pay the bill. "I can't believe I forgot again!" she said to herself on the way home. "I feel so stupid!" She planned to do it the next morning and hoped Brad wouldn't ask about it. When he did, she reacted defensively.

At the same time, Brad knew Jessica had been overloaded with work. He figured she hadn't had time to pay the bill, so he thought he could take care of it on his way to the gym the next morning. When he asked about it, he was hoping she would express her need for him and ask for comfort and assistance.

Asking for help was not easy for Jessica, and Brad was not good at voicing appreciation or taking initiative in caring for her. He wanted to feel needed, and she wished to be cared for.

The circumstance provided a perfect opportunity for each to stretch and fulfill the longing of the other, which they both wished to do. At the same time, each could have their own needs met—Brad to feel needed by offering support and compassion to Jessica, and Jessica to feel cared for by requesting Brad's help. As is often the case, however, the perfect opportunity for connection also presents a perfect scenario for misunderstanding, activating insecurity and irritation.

As they lay in silence on opposite sides of the bed, Jessica and Brad both wondered how they could feel so alienated from one another. Each knew of their own efforts to be a good marriage partner, but neither felt appreciated or valued. Each felt misunderstood and unfairly judged.

Truth is, both had looked forward to coming home that evening and letting down their guard. They felt beaten up by the world and needed encouragement and safety at home. They wanted to spend time together and enjoy the tenderness that had been so easy in the early days of their relationship.

Now both felt a combination of sadness and anger, along with confusion and waves of despair.

What do you do when you end up on opposite sides of the bed, or merely on opposite sides of an issue? How do you recover? How do you reconnect and move on?

It isn't easy, but studies reveal that couples with healthy mechanisms for resolving conflict are the most likely to make it in the long haul of marriage. Obviously, many of them don't learn how to negotiate conflict and end up on opposing sides of the bench in divorce court. There, some of the conflicts will be resolved, but at great cost and seldom to anyone's liking.

Sparring and Sparks

Romantic love is often ignited when we find ourselves attracted to one who embodies what we lack. There is truth in the old saying, "Opposites attract." If you think about it, the differences in anatomy between husband and wife provide the points of engagement for some of our most intimate encounters. But it is not only in sexual intimacy or in the attraction between us that differences are important; these differences can activate powerful negative feelings as well. Yet couples able to express the full range of negative emotions in their marriage will more likely maintain the spark of intimacy between them in the bedroom.

The opposite holds true as well. Couples that avoid conflict altogether and squelch negative feelings may enjoy a placid relationship, but they often end up relating more as roommates than as lovers. Being amiable is good as long as we also maintain authenticity. If we lose connection with our true feelings, we can't share ourselves unreservedly with our mate.

The lack of awareness or transparency about deep feelings may lead to superficiality in a relationship. If we do not learn *"speaking the truth in love"* (Ephesians 4:15), we may be guilty of withholding our hearts from one another and thus stifling growth in the marriage. Even worse, withheld negative emotions can accumulate and fill up our emotional reservoir, crowding out the positive feelings. Over time, our hearts may harden, leading to complete disconnection. *"Better is open rebuke than hidden love"* (Proverbs 27:5).

As noted before, conflict avoidance may prime us for an affair. When the wall between us grows, our union may be threatened. And when we can't see a way to remove the barriers to intimacy, they accumulate. As they mount up, we may be tempted to consider the notion that "the grass is greener on the other side of the fence."

No matter how much we like the idea of a conflict-free marriage, it is a pipe dream. The reality is that we cannot squelch negative feelings without dampening the positive ones, too. As we talk ourselves out of all our negative feelings, we may find that we have talked ourselves into not caring.

Ironically, though, we must not care so much that the idea of upsetting our mate is intolerable. This fuels much conflict avoidance. We all want a happy mate, but ultimate happiness requires a willingness to address all those things that prevent our connection. We must be willing to cause some discomfort and frustration, asking of our partner and ourselves that which we would ask of our kids. "Eat your broccoli! It's good for you."

Effective conflict resolution is vital for long-term satisfaction in marriage. Couples that go the distance and enjoy the ride have learned through trial and error how to work together as a team. Fortunately, we can learn from them, from counselors, from researchers who study marriage, and from God's Word how to play with the fires of conflict without getting burned. We need a safe way to proceed, and *Take It to the Cross* provides it. Whether you are shouting or shut down, the tool you'll learn here will help you quench conflict and ignite intimacy.

You Are a Baby!

When we cross the threshold into marriage we believe we are marrying a grown-up. But ironically, this step of maturity activates all our infantile desires. In marriage, we wish to feel perfectly cared for, completely understood, and deeply desired. We want uninterrupted attention and attunement along with absolute autonomy and freedom to be just as we are.

Like an infant with a mother, we become exquisitely sensitive to our mate and can feel desperate when our bids for attention go unheeded. The tremendous investment of emotional energy makes us feel like babies again, with a sense that we will die if we are not cared for properly. So when our connection seems threatened, we can go off the rails with agitation or anxiety or shut down and withdraw in protective isolation.

This is why conflict in marriage can be so difficult. The stakes are enormous and our desire to be heard is huge. With our personalities, priorities and perspectives so divergent that it seems at times we are not even speaking the same language, conflict can seem insurmountable.

Whose Idea Was This, Anyway?

God's intention for marriage is that two become one. It is an exciting and frightening proposition. It is not enough for us to coexist and give each other space, although that is important. To experience true oneness, we must come to terms with our differences, embrace them and search for win-win possibilities.

Because romantic love is ignited when we find someone who embodies what we lack, the stage is set for conflict. The very differences that are attractive and endearing in the beginning often provoke irritation and pain over time. The differences that once captured our hearts now stimulate our insecurities. While our partner seemed to know in the beginning how to turn us on and light us up like a Christmas tree, now it seems they know just how to push our buttons to set us off like a rocket or make us crash and burn.

In fact, for many of us, a major source of dissatisfaction is that we do not like the person we have become in relating to our mate. We become reactive, and our behavior falls far short of the ideal. To restore harmony, we need help getting back to a respectful and loving place. Our hard hearts must soften, and we must be willing to ditch our negative habits and learn skills for addressing conflict well. There is always hope when there is willingness to change.

Of course, it seems unfair that we find ourselves linked with someone who seems determined to move in a direction contrary to our own inclination. We become frustrated when our mate brings out the worst in us. Yet this appears to be the plan. Marriage, and the conflict that ensues, is a part of God's great plan to transform us. It seems He designed marriage to reveal all our junk and then help us deal with it. The great news is that the more of our junk God clears out, the more space we have in our hearts for love to flourish. Life with God is all about learning to love, and marriage is a part of what He uses to instruct us.

Of course, marriage is not the only source of conflict in our lives. Even our love relationship with God Himself is fraught with a certain measure of conflict and confusion. He makes it clear, *"My thoughts are not your thoughts, neither are your ways my ways," declares the LORD. "As the heavens are higher than the earth, so are my ways higher than your ways and my thoughts than your thoughts."* (Isaiah 55:8-9). Obviously, that vast disparity can produce some hefty conflict! One might even make a case for irreconcilable differences. However, God is all about reconciliation. Despite our inability to understand him fully, He wants to be in harmony with us, and He wants peace for our marriages, too. While it may seem impossible, *"with God all things are possible"* (Matthew 19:26).

Character and Conflict

Every good story has its share of conflict. In fact, character and conflict are what we find at the heart of any great novel, play, or movie. No one would watch reality shows if everyone got along! Imagine "Star Wars" without the wars or *Pride and Prejudice* without the tension between Darcy and Elizabeth. Without well-developed characters and clearly defined conflict, a story is boring.

Similarly, sports depend on conflict for us to get engrossed at a deep level. The greater the conflict, the more compelling the event. We want to see athletes who bring their all to the struggle of competition. We want to see heart, and we love it when opponents are equally matched. The uncertainty of the outcome grabs our attention, and we enjoy the drama as the conflict unfolds. We are inspired when teams engage with determination and character in the face of strong opponents or when they suffer defeat.

Indeed, conflict reveals and forges character. Consider Abraham Lincoln. The "War Between the States" created the necessity and the opportunity for him to shine as a bright light in a dark time. For us, as for him, conflict shows what we are made of. It brings us to moments of truth and decision. It forces us to clarify our values and declare our stand. It challenges us to take a look at who we are and what we may become. Conflict moves us. In its grip, we are faced with a choice. Will we grow, or will we regress?

We can either engage or withdraw, but conflict is a part of our journey. If we stay the course and see conflict as an opportunity to grow in character, our hearts are enlarged and our relationships strengthen. God intends for each of us to be first-string players in the game of life, lead actors in the drama that unfolds. He lets us call certain critical plays and even gives us opportunity to be co-author of our story along with Him.

The dialogue, the action, and the resolution depend largely on how each of us responds to the conflicts we encounter. Admittedly, conflict makes life difficult, but it also makes life dynamic and rewarding. Conflict adds interest to any story. God knows this, and He is anything but boring.

You don't get to decide to avoid conflict altogether, unless you choose to avoid life. If you wrap yourself in enough comfort and numb yourself to the needs of those around you, you may be able to live with comparatively little conflict. But then you will find yourself living without much adventure and missing out on a lot of joy. While you may avoid some pain, you will also rob your life of meaning. And when you opt out of playing, you can't win the game. We must be willing to suffer to see the glory of God and to secure all He intended for us.

Rewards for Avoiding Conflict

There are rewards for avoiding conflict, no doubt. In a particular moment, avoiding conflict may make perfect sense. Consider Carla and Tim.

"Don't get me started!" Carla said when Tim mentioned the clothes on the couch in the den. "You have no idea what my day has been like!" Wisely, Tim changed the subject. "So, how did your presentation go today?"

That moment, for Tim and Carla, will be better by avoiding rather than engaging an unpleasant reality. After all, Proverbs 19:11 tells us, *"A man's wisdom gives him patience; it is to his glory to overlook an offense."* It is a worthwhile skill to absorb the shock of conflict internally and thus maintain a loving and open posture in the face of difficulty. It feels good to be sturdy in that way, making allowances for others even when it inconveniences us.

In other instances, though, avoiding tension in relationship is not ideal. Yet even when we know we need to address a problem, we are tempted to sidestep it, simply because the moment at hand is less stressful if we put off engaging the issue.

So why ever do it? Why spoil a moment by bringing the source of conflict to the fore? Because all the moments that follow will be sweeter when we've swallowed our bitter pill.

The decision to take unpleasant medication makes sense if we know it will make us healthy and whole. As a doctor, I prescribe medicines that are costly and can cause unpleasant side effects, but I have seen these medications be remarkably effective and helpful. In the same way, the expense and potential side effects of facing conflict may not seem worth it. Yet in the long haul, the benefit of pressing through the discomfort far exceeds the trouble and cost. Confronting the sickness in our relationships can lead us to the cure.

Enter the Danger!

Being able to address sensitive issues opens intimacy. It is a powerful experience to speak freely without fear of rejection. Obviously, simply letting loose with everything that enters our heads can be damaging and scary. But finding a way to be forthright about difficult topics in a sensitive and constructive way is essential for growth and oneness.

In his groundbreaking book, *Emotional Intelligence*, Daniel Goleman demonstrated that the ability to engage conflict in light of long-term gain is an essential feature of emotional maturity. He cites a study done with four-year-olds, in which interviewers created internal conflict for the children by placing a marshmallow on a plate in the interview room. The child was told that the marshmallow was his and that he could eat it at will. However, the young child was also told that if he would wait a few minutes until the interviewer returned, he would be rewarded with an additional marshmallow.

Some children gobbled the marshmallow without hesitation, while others found ways to manage their impulses and resist the urge for short-term gain. They whistled or paced or even slapped their own hand as they reached for the tempting squishy white treat. In return for managing their temporary discomfort, though, they got the promised reward—two marshmallows!

This simple experiment demonstrated a profound difference between those who chose immediate gratification over long-term gain. When the two groups were compared fourteen years later, the group that gobbled rather than managed internal conflict fared poorly in life when compared to the other group. Academically, socially and behaviorally, the ability to rein in impulses and manage conflict was a huge advantage. We suffer if we fail to engage conflict or if we handle it poorly. (Goleman, Daniel. *Emotional Intelligence*. New York: Bantam, 1997. Print.)

The Rewards of Clean Conflict

"I can't believe you left the toilet seat up again!" Julie moaned.

"What's the big deal?" Bill turned toward his wife. "Can't you put it down as easily as me?"

"You know I hate turning the light on when I get up at night and I don't like groping to see if it is safe to sit. Besides, I don't like to touch it!"

"It's not that big a deal, Julie!"

"Then why don't you do it?"

Bill and Julie had hashed this through before. Though both agreed it was not a huge issue, it really bothered Julie. She decided to ask Bill to *Take It to the Cross*. They had learned the tool at a pre-marriage workshop I taught at the church and found it useful in addressing their finances.

Julie went first. When she got to **What I Think**, it dawned on her that the issue with Bill related to her childhood. She shared with him how it felt for her as a young girl sharing a bathroom with her brothers. She thought they were gross and inconsiderate. They didn't clean the sink or the tub. It seemed they never returned the seat to the down position. Sometimes they didn't aim well, and she was the one who had to clean the bathroom. When she complained, her mother consistently defended her brothers. Julie felt disregarded and disrespected. She felt she was fighting a losing battle.

As she expressed her thoughts and feelings to Bill, it became clear that the intensity of her emotion had a lot to do with those early experiences. For her, the position of the toilet seat was symbolic of her position in the family and of the fact that her mother believed women should defer to men. Julie realized that when Bill disregarded her request, she felt like a second-class citizen. Feeling as though she was married to one of her inconsiderate brothers, it was easy to see why she wouldn't want to climb back into bed and snuggle up to Bill.

Bill's perspective shifted as he heard Julie's heart. He saw that lowering the toilet seat was a concrete way to show respect for his wife, so he had a strong incentive for change. As he took his turn using the *Cross* as his guide, he told Julie he wanted her to have a different experience with him than she had growing up with her brothers. Hearing that it might enhance her tender feelings toward him also sounded promising. Through their conversation, Bill was convinced—not that Julie was right, but that she had a right to her feelings. Clearly, he could honor them by changing his behavior. Understanding her better made it easy.

Knowing Self

As Julie found, engaging conflict heightens self-awareness. Looking for the source of inner conflict often leads to discovery of deep longings and great fears. Conflict reveals core values and needs. In its grip we find what moves us to action. Who or what is in control?

Looking beneath the surface, we begin to plumb the depths of our hearts. Taking conflict to the *Cross* invites the Holy Spirit to engage the process with us. He can reveal the good, the bad, and the ugly in a gentle and loving way. We supply willingness and curiosity, allowing Him to shine a light on our souls.

Of course, self-awareness is not always pleasant. Sometimes what we find is immature or selfish. Sometimes it is embarrassing to admit insecurities or dreams. We may fear humiliation by what is revealed. Taking it to the *Cross* exposes us.

To some degree, vulnerable communication always asks us to die to self and self-protection. Many a husband would sooner take a bullet for his wife than open up the tender places in his heart. Nevertheless, this is what God asks, so that we can come together. Just as a woman must overcome her shyness about her body and sexuality, we men must relinquish our self-protective urge and bare our souls for the purpose of oneness.

"Husbands, love your wives, just as Christ loved the church and gave himself up for her" (Ephesians 5:25). This is death to self at its best—death to pride, to stoicism, to cynicism and fear, death to deception, to stonewalling, to strong-arming, isolation, and

timidity. Being vulnerable requires tremendous strength! It takes a big person to be small.

Knowing Others

Not only can healthy conflict give opportunity to know ourselves, it brings enhanced awareness and understanding of another. Bill knew Julie was the only girl in her family. He saw how her brothers still enjoyed giving her a hard time, but until he and Julie addressed the toilet seat issue, he didn't know the full story. He had no idea how deeply she had been wounded by the lack of validation from her mother. He felt a new tenderness and closeness toward her, and he admired her strength in standing up to them now. Happy to have this window opened to her past, he determined to give Julie and their daughter a different message about what it means to be a woman.

God wants to know us, and He wants us to know one another. Naturally, greater understanding means greater intimacy. On the Day of Judgment the "goats" will be sent away with the terrible truth, *"I don't know you"* (Matthew 25:12). If we are not willing to bare our soul to another person for the sake of love, we will not likely engage successfully with God. *"For anyone who does not love his brother, whom he has seen, cannot love God, whom he has not seen"* (1 John 4:20).

God's heart is for intimacy and vulnerability. *Take It to the Cross* provides a concrete means to further His purpose in our hearts and lives.

Resistance

Working through certain issues with *Take It to the Cross* can be exceptionally difficult for you or your partner at times. You may feel as if you are trudging through mud or having to pull teeth to get your partner to approach the tool with a positive attitude. Or perhaps you are the one showing resistance.

As noted before, fear and pride are often at the root of refusal to try. Admittedly, going through the steps will feel strange, funny, and a little awkward at first. You might feel like you are playing hopscotch or emotional Twister, but don't give up.

Feeling silly and unnatural is part of the process that will lead to openness. Playing a game is much better than fighting a battle. Even when life gets hectic, make time for you and your partner. Taking the time to walk through the *Cross* will pay off if you stick with it.

If identifying emotions is difficult for you or your partner, I suggest using a "feeling" chart as you both walk through the *Cross*. Telling your spouse, "I hate when you leave the kitchen messy," doesn't fully reveal how that behavior affects you. Does a sinking sensation of disappointment or hurt, frustration, or anxiety surface when the kitchen is messy? Being able to identify and voice specific feelings is important because your partner will likely show you compassion if you share your pain. Revealing concealed and tender feelings will open the doors of understanding.

When you cannot tap into your emotions, they build up inside and will surface eventually. Consider Cain from the book of Genesis. When his offering to God did not get a favorable response, Cain was upset. His face revealed his displeasure, so God invited him to talk about it. But instead of hashing it out with his Heavenly Father, Cain declined. He wasn't willing to relinquish control, so shame, hurt, and disappointment turned to anger, which he directed at his brother, Abel. Rather than use his words, Cain acted out his feelings by killing Abel.

When we don't take control of our emotions, they end up controlling us. As author Daniel Siegel encourages us, "Name it to tame it." Putting words to feelings helps us deal with them effectively. When we don't express emotions verbally, they are likely to leak out in destructive ways. (Siegel, Daniel J. *Mindsight: The New Science of Personal Transformation*. New York: Bantam, 2010. Print.)

Trusting God

Trusting that God is in control is huge in generating peace. Suspecting that someone else is in charge leaves us insecure, jockeying for position. Without confidence in God's sovereignty, conflict tempts us to assert our own dominion and grab for what we can.

By faith, however, we remind ourselves that God will ultimately have his way with us and with others. In Isaiah 46:11-12, God says it well, *"What I have said, that I will bring about; what I have planned, that I will do. Listen to me, you stubborn-hearted, you who are now far from my righteousness."* He is clear. He will have the last word. Sooner or later, we will all come around. As we internalize this truth, we can relax and give up our crusade to force others to do what we believe to be right.

The only healthy way to approach conflict is to die to our desire for control. In our effort to feel secure, we sometimes assume our way of doing things is the best way. But as we recognize and honor the kingdom of God, we can stop trying to establish the kingdom of self. My wife senses when I start trying to play God by pushing or manipulating, and she resists it. Good thing.

Living on Purpose

Facing conflict head-on is an excellent way to live with intention. It helps us be deliberate in how we spend our resources and our time. Avoiding conflict, by contrast, leaves us swept along by the flow of life, putting off decisions until they are made for us. In the words of Harvey Cox, "Not to decide is to decide." (*On Not Leaving It to the Snake* (1967))

The word "decide" is from the Latin word *decidere*. It means "to cut away." Engaging conflict by using *Take It to the Cross* helps us make decisions that cut away the things that are robbing us of well-being as a couple. We do well to cut away things that weigh us down. Material things, obligations, activities, pastimes, worries, and obsessions can sap our energy and detract from our sense of purpose. They can be like tumors draining our health and vitality. Many of our possessions and projects rob us of time and energy necessary to attend to what is most important to us.

When we take issues to the *Cross*, we are challenged to clarify our priorities and goals. We are moved to make decisions—decisions that align our behavior with what we say we value most. The process of cutting away is painful, but the reward is great. The removal of a tumor brings life and health.

In *My Utmost for His Highest*, Oswald Chambers reminds us,

"The good is always enemy of the best." (Chambers, Oswald, and James Reimann. *My Utmost for His Highest: Selections for Every Day.* Grand Rapids, MI: Discovery House, 1995. Print.)

If we simply go with the flow, we are likely to miss out on the best things in life. The highest good comes by nurturing our relationship with one another and with God - being open, intentional, and vulnerable.

Vulnerability and Worth

Healthy conflict fosters emotional and spiritual growth through disciplined listening, reflection, curiosity, honesty, and transparency. Research professor and author, Brené Brown, claims that in order to believe you are worthy of love and belonging, you must make yourself vulnerable. Try as you might, you cannot avoid conflict by trying to be perfect or by believing how you act does not affect others. Ignoring negative emotions and denying problems does not cut it. (For an excellent introduction to Dr. Brown's work, watch her TED talk on "Vulnerability")

The stimulus of conflict invites vulnerability. It is not easy to say things that will likely hurt those we love or to give them the ability to hurt us. But facing our fears is the only way to master them. Essayist and poet, Ralph Waldo Emerson, issues an unflinching challenge, "Always do what you are afraid to do."

Change requires courage. Conflict about important issues is vital, for it compels us to reveal deep and sensitive information. Let yourself be exposed in the presence of your partner. When you uncover the uncomfortable truths in your heart, you may be met with compassion and discover a shift in the relationship—one that lets you both settle in for a closer and more comforting connection.

Indeed, unresolved pain from the past often fuels intense conflict in marriage. Many of us only revisit and divulge painful childhood experiences when they are activated by current concerns. The consequences of withholding truth at some point become more damaging and painful than the potential harm of openness. Using *Take It to the Cross* helps relieve the initial sting of delivering or receiving hard truths. Conflict can bring urgency and create necessity for laying it all on the table.

We must not fall victim to the myth that vulnerability is synonymous with weakness. Quite the contrary, being undefended reveals that we are willing to risk all for a better life. Our obedience to transparent and truthful living is an act of trusting God— trusting that through imitation of His character, we will bear the fruits of His Spirit and experience the full and satisfying life Jesus came to give.

This trust in God makes it possible to risk. While God's faithfulness to our relationships is not a reward, the greater our faith, the more opportunities we have to see Him come through for us. Our confidence must not reside primarily in ourselves or in our mate. Ultimately, we depend on God to meet our needs, even—and especially—in those moments when our marriage partner does not.

Repentance and Forgiveness

In the Bible, the Greek word we translate repentance is *metanoia*. While metamorphosis is a change in shape, *metanoia* refers to a change in the way we think about something. It is an inner transformation, a realignment of thoughts and attitudes, which shows up as behavioral change. It may help to think of it as a paradigm shift, which radically affects the way we see things. Repentance is more than regret. It moves us forward into transformation rather than keeping us stuck in the past. Regret can drag us down or paralyze us. Repentance is activating.

When Bill understood Julie's feelings regarding the toilet seat, he repented that he had not taken her complaint more seriously. He regretted they had not resolved the issue sooner. And he was ready to relate differently to her in their partnership. *Take It to the Cross* promoted a shift in perception and belief, which interrupted old patterns and led to heartfelt transformation.

Repentance should be a common thing for us. We should have plenty of practice saying, "I am sorry. I was wrong. Please forgive me." Turning from old ways to new gets easier with practice. Childlike humility and openness greatly assist the process.

As Bill learned how he affected Julie, he also became clear about why he had resisted her pleas. Her complaints about the toilet seat had felt like nagging to him. He felt belittled and made wrong for leaving the toilet seat up. This felt like control, so—like most of us—he pushed back. Further, as he walked the *Cross*, he realized Julie's approach sometimes seemed parental. He did not like the feeling of having a finger wagged in his face, as if he were a "bad little boy."

When Bill relayed his thoughts and feelings to Julie, it was her turn to have her conscience educated about how she affected him. Her change of heart led her to apologize. Bill found it easy to grant her request for forgiveness, especially since he now understood the source of her frustration.

"To understand all is to forgive all," an old French proverb asserts. This does not always hold, but it is certainly true that we can feel compassion much more easily when we know someone's story. *Take It to the Cross* helps us tell our story, and it provides structure to assist us in being still and receptive as we open our hearts to hear one another.

CHAPTER 2

SAFETY FIRST: RULES OF ENGAGEMENT

Many couples come for counseling because of conflict. Despite strong commitments to marriage and children, they are unable to handle disagreements without hurting one another. After years of unproductive fighting, Dan and Lisa were ready to call it quits. Fortunately, they knew that divorce attorneys would cost a lot more than a few sessions with me, so they decided it was time to seek help for their volatile relationship.

It was clear from our first meeting that both Lisa and Dan were strongly opinionated and willing to say what they thought. They were both bright and articulate. Unfortunately, they often hurt or angered one another. In their hostile verbal exchanges each told the other exactly what they were thinking and feeling. It wasn't pretty!

After getting a little background information, including how they met and how long they had been married, I asked my usual first session opener: "If you had to put into a sentence or two why you made this appointment, what would you say?"

Dan spoke up. "We fight all the time. I thought we could fix our own problems, but last week I got so mad I threw a vase against a wall."

"Ouch! I guess that got your attention!" I glanced at Lisa and then back at Dan. "Well, what do you argue about?"

"Everything, Paul—money, disciplining the kids, you name it. We're at opposite ends of the spectrum. It's like we disagree about everything. Almost every subject leads to a fight."

"But you've been married fourteen years, something must be working," I observed.

"Well, we have great sex," Dan smiled broadly. "She is obviously hot. And we do love our kids."

Lisa chimed in, "Yeah, and he has a cute butt."

"Well, I guess that's a start," I grinned. "What happens when you disagree?"

"One or the other of us usually gets loud," Lisa replied, "then we are off and running. Sometimes I think we are just addicted to conflict. It's a habit, the way we do business. We fight, release a little tension, we make up or move on, and then we go at it again."

Dan agreed. "It's true. We both know it's only a matter of time until the next eruption."

"Sounds like the Old Faithful geyser in Yellowstone Park. It's predictable, but you don't want to be standing too close when it goes off.

"Do your conflicts ever solve anything?" I asked. "Do you come away with an acceptable compromise?"

After thinking for a moment, both shook their heads.

"No," Dan said. "One of us just gives in and we go on or put the issue on hold until we have another fight."

"Wow. It sounds like you guys fight way too much. Hmmm… maybe Lisa needs to be a little less 'hot,' and Dan needs to be less of a 'butt,'" I smiled broadly.

Both laughed and nodded agreement. "So," I asked, "can you ever remember working through an issue to the point you came up with a solution you both felt good about?"

After a pause, both Dan and Lisa again shook their heads.

Amazingly, this is typical. Many couples tell me they have never successfully resolved an issue to the point that both felt satisfied. Rather than "win-win" solutions, most couples experience round after round of "win-lose" interactions. It is no wonder they slip into adversarial postures and get entrenched in terrible power struggles.

But Dan and Lisa were sick of fighting. Both were ready for some tangible assistance, and I was happy to reassure them I could help with an effective conflict-resolution tool. First, though, I suggested they could do with a little safety course. Like the "STOP, DROP, and ROLL" technique we teach kids to practice in case they ever catch fire, we all need strategies to employ when a relationship bursts into flames.

Fortunately, teaching children to practice "STOP, DROP, and ROLL" actually prevents tragic injury and saves lives. By the same token, learning safety practices for conflict can also spare us suffering if we are willing to practice.

For Dan and Lisa, I suggested a few ground rules and gave them a written copy, entitled, "Ground Rules for Fighting Fair."

- Set a time limit for discussion.
- Address only one problem at a time.
- Use "I" statements whenever possible.
- Keep the volume low. No name-calling or profanity.
- No hatefulness or hitting "below the belt".
- No aggressive gestures such as finger pointing or invading another's space.
- Avoid making judgments, and avoid using the words "always" and "never."
- No arguing or discussing sensitive issues after 8:30 PM.
- No negative conversations in bed.
- Either partner can call a time-out if things start to escalate, and the other must back off.
- Re-engage the conversation after an agreed-upon cooling off period.

Both Lisa and Dan agreed to try these limits in their difficult discussions, so I asked them to sign and date their copy, and to post it at home where they could easily reference it.

These ground rules helped them avoid some destructive patterns in their marriage, and they learned to stick with one problem at a time. They learned to monitor their tone of voice and impulsive reactions when addressing problems.

I also shared the Speaker—Listener Technique as found in the excellent book *A Lasting Promise: The Christian Guide to Fighting for Your Marriage.* (Stanley, Scott. A Lasting Promise: A Christian Guide to Fighting for Your Marriage. San Francisco: Jossey-Bass, 1998. Print.

The Speaker-Listener Technique

"Take note of this: Everyone should be quick to listen, slow to speak, and slow to become angry, for man's anger does not bring about the righteous life that God desires" (James 1: 19-20).

Rules for Both of You

1. ***The Speaker has the floor.*** Use a real object to designate the floor. You can use anything, the TV remote, a piece of paper, a paperback book, anything at all. If you do not have the floor, you are the Listener. Note that the Speaker keeps the floor while the Listener paraphrases, keeping it clear who is in which role all the time.

2. ***Share the floor.*** You share the floor over the course of a conversation. One has it to start and may say a number of things. At some point, you switch roles, and continue back and forth as the floor changes hands.

3. ***No problem solving.*** When using this technique you are going to focus on having good discussions. You must consciously avoid coming to solutions prematurely.

Rules for the Speaker

1. ***Speak for yourself.*** Don't mind-read. Talk about your thoughts, feelings, and concerns, not your perceptions or interpretations of the Listener's point of view or motives. Try to use "I" statements, and talk about your own point of view.

2. ***Talk in small chunks.*** You will have plenty of opportunity to

say all you need to say, so you don't have to say it all at once. It is very important to keep what you in manageable pieces to help the Listener actively listen. A good rule of thumb is to keep your statements to just a sentence or two, especially when first learning the technique.

3. ***Stop and let the Listener paraphrase.*** After saying a bit, perhaps a sentence or two, stop and allow the Listener to paraphrase what you just said. If the paraphrase was not quite accurate, you should politely restate what was not heard in the way it was intended to be heard. Your goal is to help the Listener hear and understand your point of view.

Rules for the Listener

1. ***Paraphrase what you hear.*** To paraphrase the Speaker, briefly repeat back what you heard the Speaker say, using your own words if you like, to make sure you understand what was said. The key is that you show your partner that you are listening as you restate what you heard, without any interpretations. If the paraphrase is not quite right (which happens often), the Speaker should gently clarify the point being made. If you truly don't understand some phrase or example, you may ask the Speaker to clarify or repeat, but you may not ask question on any other aspect of the issue unless you have the floor.

2. ***Don't rebut. Focus on the Speaker's message.*** While in the Listener role, you may not offer your opinion or thoughts. This is the hardest part of being a good Listener. If you are upset by what your partner says, you need to edit out any response you may want to make, so you can continue to pay attention to what your partner is saying. Wait until you get the floor to state your response. As Listener, your job is to speak only in the service of understanding your partner. Any words or gestures to show your own opinions are not allowed, including making faces. Your task is to understand. Good listening does not equal agreement. You can express any disagreement when you have the floor.

Check-in Time

As I do with many couples, I suggested Dan and Lisa set a time to meet each week to check in with one another. Sunday evening, I told them, is often a good time to review the previous week and look forward to the one ahead. As an aid to looking back, I recommended they use the Speaker-Listener Technique and take turns sharing their view of the prior few days. What were the high points? When did they seem to hit rock bottom?

They could also use the time to check in with themselves to clear away any ill feelings they had not communicated or been able to shake. After each had a backward look using the technique, they could together look ahead and plan for times to connect emotionally, playfully, spiritually, and sexually. "If you don't plan for connection," I told them, "it may not happen."

New Pathways for Peace

Dan and Lisa learned to listen attentively as their partner shared desires, feelings, thoughts, and proposals, and then to take turns expressing themselves honestly and completely. They became skilled at reflecting back understanding and recommitted daily to the process of growing together in love.

Over several sessions, they became more vulnerable and receptive to one another. They stopped blaming and began to look at things from a loving, rather than a legal, point of view. Watching them experience grace for one another and find a new level of peace within was beautiful. New possibilities opened up in their relationship as they began to experience better cooperation. They also defined some clear-cut domains in their marriage.

Not only were they getting along better, their children were fighting less and helping more. The ground rules for Dan and Lisa impacted all the interactions in their home. Even their physical surroundings became less chaotic, reflecting the new peace and harmony they were promoting. The fresh dynamic of respect and cooperation began permeating every area of their lives.

Safety First

Just like Dan and Lisa, we can all use some guidelines for important relationships. We need the promise of safety to fully let down our guard. And since conflict taps into powerful emotions, using restraint is important when communicating at a deep level. We want to speak truth, but we need to do it in love. Some of the suggested ground rules are obvious. No name-calling. Pejorative terms are demeaning and cause separation rather than bringing us together.

Loudness often feels hostile and aggressive, and can incite defensiveness in our partner. Keeping the volume low demonstrates self-control and respect for self and other. A raised voice can activate the fight-flight mechanism, which moves us from receptive, reflective mode to action mode. Blood moves away from the brain into the body and limits our capacity for a calm and rational response.

Remember that your experience and your mate's may be radically different. When Teri says, "Stop yelling at me," I have to remind myself that she is exquisitely sensitive to a raised tone because of the trauma inflicted by a bipolar mother. While to my ears my tone sounds nothing like yelling, I can agree to change my behavior even when I don't agree with her assessment.

Judgmental statements should be avoided completely. "You are so selfish! You only care about yourself." "It's never enough with you! You are never satisfied." "You are only saying that to get on my good side." "That's not really how you feel!" "You are just like your mother!" "You are such a loser!" "You are not even trying to understand!" "That's ridiculous!" "You are impossible!"

Contrary to the old rhyme that declares, "Sticks and stones can break my bones, but words can never hurt me," words do have tremendous power for harm. *The tongue has the power of life and death, and those who love it will eat its fruit*" (Proverbs 18:21).

We can tell our partner how we experience them, but the words we choose can make all the difference. "Sometimes it seems you care about no one but yourself." "I feel like I am carrying the whole burden of managing our finances." "You don't seem at all concerned with my needs." "Sometimes it looks as if you tune me out." Sharing how others come across to us and how we feel about them brings understanding. Using "I" statements shows we are taking responsibility for our feelings and doing our best to give useful feedback. A judgment begs to be argued, while an observation invites closer inspection.

A helpful format for sharing is to say, "When you _____ [name the specific action in the specific situation], I feel _____ [name the specific emotion]." For example, "When you interrupt me when we are out with friends, I feel disrespected and ignored."

If there is defensiveness, affirming one's perspective without presuming to be right can go a long way toward effective communication and resolution. "I hope I am wrong, but this is how it appears to me." Again, we ought not pass judgment. *"Do not judge, or you too will be judged"* (Matthew 7:1). Judgments move interactions from heart to head. *Take It to the Cross* is not about building a case or laying down the law. On the contrary, it is about dismantling defenses. We want to be loving, not legal!

Similarly, criticism will provoke a defensive response. John Gottman, prominent researcher in couples' communications, distinguishes between complaint and criticism. In his book, *The Seven Principles for Making Marriage Work*, he notes that a *complaint* focuses attention on a behavior or problem, where *criticism* is directed at the person. (Gottman, John Mordechai., and Nan Silver. *The Seven Principles for Making Marriage Work.* New York: Crown, 1999. Print.)

Statements focused on personal feelings that arise in response to a mate's behavior are much more likely to be heard than judgments about those same behaviors. Listen to the difference between the approach styles below:

- "I am angry and hurt because you forgot to do what I asked of you. Sometimes it feels like you are oblivious to my needs. I want to believe you care for me, but sometimes I fear that you don't."
- "I can't believe you forgot again! You never listen to me. You obviously don't care about anyone but yourself!"

In the first approach, the speaker is focused on personal experience and fears. In the second communication, the speaker crosses a line by pronouncing judgment. He or she voices an accusation, endorsing a negative interpretation of the partner's behavior and casting aspersions on character. Understandably, the other partner's reaction may not be pretty, as they feel the need to defend against accusations.

It takes discipline and practice to give our partner the benefit of the doubt. But if even a tiny chance to attribute a positive motive to a behavior rather than a negative one, we do well to verbalize it. Studies show we tend to focus on our own positive motives but focus on others negative results. With attention and desire, we can override this human tendency. Verbalizing my hope about my partner's possible intention helps to balance out my fear of the worst. Don't forget that Satan was even able to cast doubt on God's intentions in the garden with Adam and Eve. The enemy always wants us to assume the worst of those we love.

If he is successful, Satan makes us believe that our mate is not really there for us. Even more, he wishes to undermine our trust in God. He wants us to opt for control over vulnerability.

Proactive Problem-Solving

It's easy to put off confrontation until we've "had it." But then when we get into conflict, we are likely bound for a bloody battleground.

As we learn to *"submit to one another out of reverence for Christ,"* (Ephesians 5:21), God's design for authority becomes clearer. We realize that the attitude of meekness is Jesus' invitation to peace. Meekness is not weakness, but rather strength under control. We submit because we love our Master, even as a gentled horse has learned to control its strength for love of its master.

We can live at peace with one another when we stop "playing God" by trying to control all our circumstances and our mate. We must be willing to surrender our desire to change our partner and stop trying to make them conform to our image. In fact, if we are willing, we can learn to appreciate the other's different perspective and the strength our differences bring to our relationship.

As I yield my expectations to God, I feel more gratitude when others do things to bless me. I learn to delay gratification and wait for God to unite us in purpose, rather than force my way. At the same time, I am not as prone to give in for the sake of harmony. By managing the tension between us more wisely, we work better as a team.

As Dan and Lisa learned to yield to one another, they found enhanced cooperation and creativity. New solutions to old problems began to open up, and they found renewed enjoyment in the differences that attracted them to one another in the beginning. Each of them could draw on their respective strengths and act as teacher for the other. By doing so, their disagreements become less threatening and were seen as opportunities for learning and growth, rather than occasions for fear. With ground rules in place, Lisa and Dan were calmer and more open to outside input as well as feedback from one another.

Through an attitude of meekness and yielding to one another, a marriage begins to offer greater returns. By observing ground rules and establishing healthy communication strategies, we feel more connected and eager to understand each other. And as we get more connected to God and submit to His authority, things work better.

Take It to the Cross Ground Rules

1. **Pray.** As important as it is to cooperate with one another, inviting God's involvement is even more crucial. The Bible tells us, *"There is a way that seems right to a man, but in the end it leads to death"* (Proverbs 16:25). Even our most brilliant notions may fall far short of God's plan for us. Fortunately, scripture tells us we can ask for wisdom, and God will give it generously (James 1:5). Whenever we approach conflict, we want to ask His aid. Pray.

2. *Set aside a time when you're both ready to engage conflict.* It's very important to voice the need. For example, "I have something I need to address. I'd like for us to make a decision about the kids schooling next year. Would you be willing to talk about it? If so, let's set a time." It can be difficult to find the time to use this tool, especially with small children at home. Look for fifteen minutes to a half an hour when you can be as focused and uninterrupted as possible. Note: "Are you willing to talk about it?" is a better

question than "Do you want to talk about it?" We are often ambivalent about addressing conflict. Willingness is more powerful than desire and can help us overcome our resistance to having difficult conversations.

3. **Stick to one issue at a time.** Many issues are inter-related, so if we're not careful, we'll end up with half a dozen issues on the table and no possibility of resolution. Be disciplined. Don't burden yourself or your partner with a laundry list of complaints to address in one session—you both will end up feeling overwhelmed and emotionally exhausted. In the process, don't let yourself say, "Oh, and while we're at it . . ." "Well, if we're going to deal with this, then I ought to be able to deal with that, too . . ." Resist the temptation. Stick with one issue.

4. **Stop when time is up.** Set a timer. When the time allotted is up, stop. Or if it's clear that you must reach an agreement, take a break. Think about what you have heard and pray for clarity and creativity. Whoever is keeping up with the time may need to take the initiative. "Okay, we need to take this up again later. When is a good time?"

Even though we are tempted to soldier through it, having time for things to settle can work wonders. Teri and I have even re-engaged an issue later, only to find that we had each been convinced by the other's communication and each had decided to defer to the other. Coming back to the issue later, we found ourselves in the happy position of arguing for the other to have their way!

Over and over, we have found making time for individual processing and prayer extremely helpful. After engaging *Take It to the Cross* together, expressed thoughts, feelings and desires can function like little seeds. As they take root and grow, they change our attitudes and perspectives. We can ask God, then, to change both of us—to bring our minds and hearts together. Oneness is His great desire for us. He can do it!

5. **Speak only when you have the floor.** When using the tool, one partner stands as the other sits at the foot of the cross. The one standing literally has the floor. The seated partner must exercise

discipline and remain silent until the speaker is finished. Then roles are reversed when the second partner stands to enjoy uninterrupted attention.

The only exception occurs when the seated partner requests clarification from the speaker. As in a classroom setting, raising a hand and waiting to be called on is an excellent protocol to follow. Being seated helps suppress the urge to jump in, but feel free to hold your hand to your mouth or use duct tape if you are tempted to speak!

Not only is it important to be silent, the seated partner must monitor their non-verbal communication, too. It is vital to demonstrate courteous attention and to avoid eye-rolling, sighing, or other negative non-verbal feedback. Alternatively, positive non-verbal feedback can encourage and empower your spouse. Body language communicates volumes!

6. *Monitor your speech.* When you have the floor, keep your volume low and tone calm and respectful. Even as body language communicates so much, tone of voice is huge in affecting the impact of the message. Use "I" statements throughout, even when addressing the other person's behavior. "Sometimes it feels to me that you just don't care," rather than, "You just don't care about me." Avoid shaming and blaming. No name-calling or coarse language.

7. *Literally walk the Cross.* While it is tempting to stand still or sit down to talk, physically moving through the process helps with focus and assists us in staying engaged. Making the actual move from one step to another makes it less likely that we fall into old patterns of defending our position, by turning away or sitting with arms folded. Standing also seems to make us more vulnerable and more in touch with emotions. When we stand, we support our own weight, literally taking a stand for our needs and desires.

Recent social science research has uncovered how holding poses that display power for even a couple of minutes can change us for the better. As an example, think of Superman or Wonder Woman. Standing with chin lifted, legs spread, and fists poised at the waist can actually change our hormone levels, making us feel more confident and thus able to speak more authentically.

Having one person stand and the other sit alters the power dynamic between them. Interrupting the usual power differential can work wonders in opening fresh possibilities for partnership and open communication. The standing partner grows in the ability to declare their heart, and the seated partner gains the power to be still and attentive, creating a calm space to encourage open discourse.

We also know that we tend to handle bad news better if we are seated. The "bad news" of our partner's perspective will be easier to take in and metabolize if we are seated comfortably. This puts us in observation mode as we make ourselves audience to our partner's unfolding drama. And taking notes reminds us of being a good student, inspiring our partner to enlighten us about the workings of their mind and heart.

We want our partner to have our full attention when they have the floor, and we want the same consideration when we speak. You will find with practice that the model works best when partners take turns standing.

In addition to these ground rules, couples may create some that are unique to their own relationship. Though rules can be modified or overlooked later, hold them rigorously in the beginning. And do guard against complacency. If old default habits become active in your discussions again, don't hesitate to reintroduce the ground rules. Like flotation devices on an aircraft, ground rules are vital when things go badly. As Dan and Lisa found, adhering to ground rules transforms the atmosphere between two people at odds. When each feels respected and understood, interactions become characterized by courtesy rather than chaos.

CHAPTER 3

HOW CONFLICT TAKES US TO THE CROSS

There are several reasons for calling this tool *"Take It to the Cross."* The tool itself consists of six pages to be arranged on the floor in the shape of a cross. Thus, we literally take our conflicts "to the cross." This is a visual of how our natural inclinations often run counter to those of others. Each time we use it, we begin in opposing positions. It demonstrates tangibly how we are "at cross-purposes" with one another and how we get closer as we walk the steps.

The cross reminds us that we must be willing to die to our own agenda, and that deep and abiding peace in relationships requires death to self. The relationship must be important enough to turn my "M" over to a "W" — surrendering "me" for "we." I can't have all I want, when I want it, if I am to be in a relationship of peace and equality. In almost every conflict, involved parties must compromise to achieve satisfying resolution.

Coming to the cross honors God's purpose and plan for us. It demonstrates awareness of our need for His wisdom and strength in approaching problems. We need Him in all our decisions, and the visual of the cross supports us in coming together. He tells us to trust Him, to acknowledge Him in our ways and not lean on our own understanding. When we do this, He promises to lead us (Proverbs 3:5-6).

Plus, the cross was God's means of setting aside the law. The law was external. Under the law, negative consequences or punishments acted as deterrents to doing wrong. Through the cross, God's aim was to replace this *external* standard and motivation with an *internal* source of strength through His Spirit inside us. In the same way, we find peace with each other when we move from legal to loving, when we stop focusing so much on external factors and share what is at the core.

We must die to a right /wrong mentality. Any argument or conversation that leads to, "Fine! You're right!" is a hollow victory. Ask yourself: "Do I want to be right, or do I want to connect?" What we long for is mutual regard and loving deference, not placation or capitulation. We want a win-win scenario, with a result we can both heartily endorse. The cross makes it possible.

Finally, we are reminded that Jesus is the peacemaker, and His willingness to go to the cross bought us peace with God. Our willingness to take our desires and conflicts to His cross will bring us peace with one another. *Take It to the Cross* moves us safely from conflict to deep connection.

This tool generates more positive feedback than any other that my wife and I share through our retreats. Couples write us years later to thank us and affirm, "Our relationship has been transformed, and we still take things to the *Cross.*"

Problems in Paradise

Dena and Kevin had both experienced the trauma of a broken marriage prior to meeting each other. Now gratefully married and fully committed to God and each other, they determined this would be the union of their dreams.

Of course, it took only a few months of married life for differences to surface and emotional garbage to accumulate. They came to our "One Flesh" marriage retreat sadly aware that the tensions they tried to hide were building daily. Conflicts were becoming unavoidable, and they had no mechanisms for resolution.

Although they had many issues, a frequent source of friction was the state of their kitchen. Kevin expected Dena to keep their house as neat as hers was when they were dating. Unfortunately, her teenage children were not in the habit of tidiness unless they were expecting guests. Now that he was no longer "company," they felt no obligation to pick up after themselves.

Kevin was particularly irritated by dirty dishes in the sink. "It only takes a minute to rinse them and put them in the dishwasher. What's so hard about that?"

Dena felt herself caught in the middle between Kevin and her children. Also, she felt unappreciated for the hours she spent cooking and cleaning for all of them.

Peacemaking, Not Peacekeeping

By keeping silent and picking up her children's things for them, Dena was trying to keep the peace. In turn, Kevin often swallowed his frustration and tried not to "rock the boat." He firmly believed that what he wanted would be good for all concerned but didn't know how to address the issue without coming across as critical and blaming. Both were aware of the strain, but open communication was hindered by an unspoken commitment to conflict avoidance.

Jesus, though, did not tell us to be peace**keepers**. He said, *"Blessed are the peace**makers**, for they shall be called sons of God"* (Matthew 5:9). The act of making peace suggests we go to the place where peace is missing, rather than avoiding it. In speaking up as a peacemaker, we learn to address issues by exposing our hearts without malice or manipulation.

Listening as a peacemaker occurs when we listen attentively, seeking to understand another's point of view well enough to put their perspective in our own words. To hear well, we must listen without interrupting and without injecting defensive comments. Such generous listening honors others and fosters understanding as we learn more about our partner's feelings and thoughts.

With a commitment to clear and honest communication, peacemakers work toward agreements that both parties can fully affirm. And when we reach resolution, we are sometimes amazed we didn't see the solution sooner.

Being a peacemaker is challenging. Recent research with couples has revealed that conflict between husband and wife often activates a strong "fight/flight" or "freeze" response. Feeling threat to the marital bond can throw our survival mechanisms into high gear, much as if we saw a rabid dog heading our way. In the face of these intense physiological responses, every cell in our bodies is primed to attack or run away. Alternatively, our brains may go into overload and shut down.

When approached by an upset partner, some of us are like "a deer in the headlights," unsure of which way to turn. Learning to remain calm in the face of threatening interactions is a huge gain, but we need tools to help us and a deep assurance that God will empower us to manage our struggles gracefully.

Without a commitment to being peacemakers, we are likely to end up as a withdrawer or a pursuer. Pursuers by nature tend to be anxious until there is resolution. They feel intense desires to hash things out, so they tend to approach their mate with high-level intensity. For anyone who has been steamrolled or deeply wounded in conflict, the intense approach is terrifying. If the intense pursuer is also a rapid verbal processer and the other needs solitude and time to process internally, they have a recipe for complete disaster.

Being convinced the "withdrawer" spouse will never want to deal with the problem, a pursuer often feels they have waited far too long. As their level of intensity about the issue peaks, they feel extreme urgency to confront their partner. For the pursuer, now is the time, and they won't let it rest until it's resolved! The withdrawer, on the other hand, instinctively resists opening up emotionally in the face of pressure, much as we tend do when feeling pressured to engage sexually with another.

Peace begins within. When we first hash things out with God, He can handle our intensity and restore peace to our souls. In this way, the pursuer's approach can be characterized by peaceful persistence rather than aggressive insistence. We must trust God with the outcome. Pursuers can minimize resistance and help a distancer mate feel calmer by asking for a good time to talk.

Getting a commitment and setting a time to talk allows both to be ready and more relaxed.

To override peacekeeping and become effective peacemakers, we husbands must learn in practical terms how to lay down our lives, setting aside our own interests and agendas. Sometimes this means stepping out of our comfort zone. Sometimes laying down our lives is as simple and as difficult as turning off the television and laying down the remote control so our wives may have our full attention. Sometimes we have to make tough choices, such as giving work a lower priority at key moments. Doing so demonstrates our commitment to being a peacemaker and infuses the marriage with a tremendous sense of value.

Wives, likewise, need a deep understanding of Christ-like submission and respect. When a husband senses prideful resistance or disrespect, he is tempted to push harder to assert his own will or to withdraw and abdicate all responsibility. At the same time, a peacemaking wife does not withhold her view. Rather, she expresses herself clearly and courageously with love and with respect. She is able to wade in and work on issues; she is also able to wait.

Children know how to make a protest. They share authentic reactions to things that others do and make it clear when they are unhappy. Even when they have little power or control, they are bold in asserting their desires and displeasure. If this boldness has become squelched in us, we may only know how to complain. This has an unfortunate effect which is very different from a strong and direct protest or request.

When we show up authentically and speak truthfully in a loving way, we experience deep and abiding peace by demonstrating our our deep commitment to intimacy. And we sense God's pleasure when our behavior is motivated by love, and we pursue deep understanding of our partner's perspective.

Submission and surrender are embodied in the *Cross*. As tempting as it is to keep the peace, learning to be a peacemaker empowers both the individuals and the partnership. Learning to speak up and courageously challenge the status quo promotes growth. Healthy marriage partners bring out the best in one another. *"As iron sharpens iron, so one person sharpens another"* (Proverbs 27:17).

TAKE IT TO THE CROSS

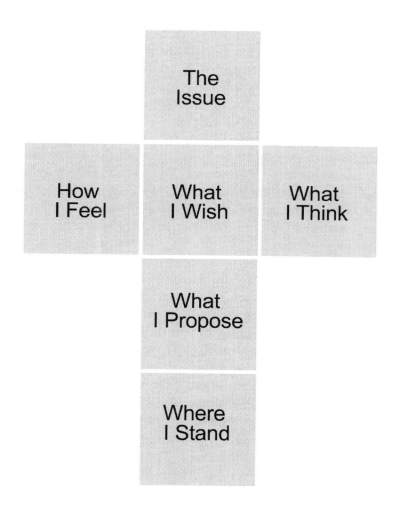

Take It to the Cross consists of a set of six laminated cards marked like the rectangles in the diagram on the opposite page. Of course, you can simply write the words on your own paper and arrange them on the floor in the shape of a cross. Or you can use the tear out pages at the back of the book.

The person who has raised the issue will usually go first, but either one can start. The person who begins is asked to stand and physically walk the cross, while the other sits silently listening.

Sitting at the foot of the cross reminds us of the source of peace and its cost. It places us in a posture of stillness and openness. Thoughtfully tuning in to our mate's presence and their communication puts us in a receptive mode, like babies taking it all in. It reminds us that a calm and peaceful presence invites others to share openly and honestly. And avoiding the temptation to defend is very disarming. It makes it possible for my mate to take the time to get it all out. And if your partner is skittish about sharing deeply, your stillness will make it feel much safer to draw near.

Standing and speaking allows us to be more vulnerable and grounded. When we take an erect posture, we are more likely to connect with our strength, our convictions, and our emotions. The opportunity to be clear and focused increases the odds of being heard, especially if we share from the heart. This is not easy, but when we do, we take a stand for the relationship.

As we identify the issue and share our wishes, fears, thoughts, and feelings, we are making an authentic bid for attention, attunement, and intimacy. Standing up while our partner sits makes it clear that we have the floor and allows us to dig deeper and stay connected with our true self. When we stand, we are less likely to take a defensive posture and more likely to stay engaged. As we bare our souls, intimacy becomes possible.

How It Works

Partner A presents: Standing at the head of the cross, partner A identifies the issue and then takes one step forward to voice his or her wish for resolving the topic in an ideal world. The arms of the cross then allow A to step to the right and acknowledge *How I Feel*, or to the left to reveal *What I Think*. Back-and-forth movement is encouraged until all of partner A's thoughts and feelings are fully explored. At that point, a step down the vertical beam of the cross gives opportunity to offer **What I Propose**. The foot of the cross allows **Where I Stand** to be declared, anchoring the whole conversation in commitment.

Partner B reflects: The partners swap positions. Partner B stands and moves to the head of the cross to review the high points of partner A's communication while partner A listens in silence. If anything significant is overlooked, partner A can jog B's memory so he or she can reiterate what was missed.

Partner B shares: Once A is satisfied that B has heard well, B now takes a turn walking the cross. The issue does not change, but it is restated. Afterward, B walks through all the stations of the cross, from **What I Wish** at the center to **How I Feel** and **What I Think** at the sides, and then down to **What I Propose** and **Where I Stand**.

Partner A reflects: As before, partners switch positions. After standing and moving back to the head of the cross, A recaps what has been related, restating the gist of B's communication. If anything important is omitted, B, now seated at the foot of the cross, can reinforce it, so A can include it in their summary back to B.

Partner A reconsiders: After satisfactory summarization of B's discourse, A can add any new thoughts or feelings and then proceed on to **What I Propose**. At this juncture, A may agree with B's proposal or amend it and then make another brief statement of commitment at **Where I Stand**.

Partner B reviews: If the proposal is not yet endorsed by both, then B takes the floor, exchanging places with A, who sits again. B recaps the new content A has shared and repeats the proposal as A presented it. If A is satisfied that B listened well, B continues.

Partner B's second time through: Like A has done, B walks the cross a second time and shares any new wishes, thoughts or feelings and then reiterates the proposal along with any modification desired and a brief recap of commitment.

Partner A's recap and proposal: A quick summary of what B just shared is followed by A's opportunity for other thoughts and an attempt to bring the proposal to a final state.

If the two are getting close to agreement, but not quite there, then it makes sense to engage one or two more rounds more to craft a proposal they both approve. But when both have made two passes and are still in strong disagreement about the proposal, it may be time to propose a break to allow further reflection, prayer, more research, or the aid of a coach of some kind. Don't worry if you have a little confusion about the process now. There is much more to come, with plenty of examples to illustrate.

Take It to the Cross in Action

At our "One Flesh" retreats, we invite a couple to identify a small disagreement that they are willing to address in front of the others. "Later," I explain, "experiencing the dynamics of the process in minor issues will make it safe to go on to more volatile problems."

Kevin and Dena offered to be our guinea pigs. With a little coaching, this is how they worked through their issue.

First we set the stage by laying the six laminated cards on the floor in the shape of a cross. Since Kevin raised the issue, he took his place standing at the head of the cross, prepared to speak. Dena was instructed to sit silently on the couch at the foot of the cross as he walked through the process. It was her job to listen attentively, and she was told she could take notes if she felt it would help her focus on his communication. She was urged to focus on what Kevin was saying and she would have her turn later. During this stage, understanding is enhanced when the listening spouse chooses not to dwell on her own view or rebuttal.

First was ***The Issue.*** Kevin stood on that card, crossed his arms, and said, "The issue is that I'm unhappy about the way our house is kept."

"That's a big issue, Kevin," I observed. "Is there one thing about the housekeeping that really bothers you? See if you can narrow it down."

"Okay. The issue is that people are too lazy to put their dishes in the dishwasher. They just pile them in the sink."

"That's focused. How about framing it more simply as: 'Dishes in the sink'?" Obviously, I wanted to steer Kevin away from any foregone conclusions that might sound like a judgment or attack.

After agreeing that was the heart of the issue, Kevin moved to the center of the cross, **What I Wish.** Here, he uncrossed his arms. "What I want is for the dishes to be rinsed and put in the dishwasher."

"That's cool," I said, "but what would it look like in your ideal world?"

He blinked. "Well, the kitchen would stay clean."

"How about this?" I asked. "I wish that the dishes would rinse themselves and jump in the dishwasher. Or maybe you could wish you and Dena had maid service. Will that ever happen? Not likely! But wishing for it lets Dena see your heart for her."

"Okay. Yeah! In an ideal world, I would wish for us to have enough money to hire you a full-time maid—make that a whole staff of servants!"

"I like it!" I said, enjoying his enthusiasm.

Stating our wish or ideal "in the perfect world" helps us accept that reality rarely allows a perfect outcome for either partner. This recognition softens us to compromise.

Next, he moved to the arms of the cross, alternating between **How I Feel** and **What I Think.**

"I feel angry when I come in the kitchen and see a sink full of dirty dishes."

Dena burst out, "There's never a sink full—maybe a glass or two!" I reminded her of her role as active listener. Her turn was coming. I also encouraged Kevin that he need not get derailed by arguing with Dena.

He moved to **thoughts.** "I think, because you've been a single mom and had to work, the kids have not been taught to keep things neat. I also think you don't know how much this bothers me." Then he went back to **feelings.** "But it really ticks me off when I come home and see glasses, cups, whatever, sitting in the sink."

Now it was time for **What I Propose.** "I propose that we put a can by the sink and fine whoever leaves the dish a quarter."

Lastly, Kevin shared from **Where I Stand.** "I love you, Dena, and am so thankful God brought you and the kids into my life. I really want to work this out." This brought him back to what was most important, his commitment to God, to his wife, and to their family.

Turnabout Is Fair Play

"Is it my turn, now?" Dena jumped to her feet, her eyes flashing. "It's not like there are dishes all over the kitchen, Kevin!"

I encouraged her to trust the process and remain as calm as possible while she shared. First, I instructed, she would restate the issue, Kevin's wish, the gist of his thoughts and feelings, and his proposal.

"Okay," she said as she stood on **The Issue** card. "The issue is dishes being left in the sink." She moved to the feelings card. "That bothers you, and you don't think I understand why." Stepping over to the **What I Think** card, Dena reiterated Kevin's view, "You think the kids haven't been trained, and you propose to teach all of us by fining us a quarter for every dish left out. Is that right?"

Kevin had taken his place at the foot of the cross, and he looked at me for permission to speak. "Yeah, that's pretty much it. Except you didn't say that I love you and am committed to a good marriage."

"Sorry," she said. "It is really important to me that you said that. Thank you for the reminder." She stepped to **Where I Stand** and restated what Kevin had clarified for her. While a bit tedious at times, the value of restating our partner's communications is extremely validating and creates a sense of attention and attunement. Our partners know we heard them.

Once she finished restating Kevin's communication, I invited Dena to walk the cross and share her own perspectives.

Dena took a deep breath, moving back to the head of the

cross. "The issue is dishes in the sink." "**What I Wish,**" she said taking a step forward, "is for you to come home and really appreciate the home I'm making for you. It's a lot better than your old bachelor pad!"

She moved to the **feelings** card. "I feel very hurt at your insinuation that I'm lazy." Tears sparkled in her eyes. "I really work hard, Kevin!"

Then she stepped sideways to the **What I Think** card. "I think there must be some other reason this bugs you, probably a leftover from your childhood. I don't think it has anything to do with reason."

Next, it was Dena's turn to take a stab at a proposal. "I don't like your proposal, Kevin. The kids are almost grown and I think we need to treat them like adults. I want them to love you. If they were treated like ten-year-olds, fined a quarter for every dirty dish, I think they would feel resentful."

"Do you have a counter-proposal?" I asked.

Standing on the **What I Propose** card, Dena thought for a moment. "I propose that since I know this is such a source of irritation for you, Kevin, I will check the kitchen before you come home at night. If a cup or a glass has been left out, I'll make sure it's put away before you come in the door."

"Can you do that without becoming resentful?" I asked.

She nodded and moved to the commitment card. "I, too, am committed to a good marriage. If it will make you happy, I don't mind doing this."

The Second Time Around

Dena sat down, and Kevin slowly stood up. This time it was he who was almost in tears. He moved immediately to **How I Feel.** "I feel—I feel bad. I am sorry I hurt your feelings, Dena. I know you're not lazy. Please forgive me?"

She nodded, and he continued. "I agree that it's irrational to worry about a few dishes. I can't explain why. I wish I could change myself and never let these small things bother me again."

For the sake of completion, I asked Kevin to go back up to the head of the cross and recap what he had heard from Dena. After doing so, she agreed that he had the main points. I invited him to share any other thoughts or feelings that had arisen. There was nothing else, so he was ready to return to **What I Propose**.

He moved to the card. "I accept your proposal, Dena. I also propose that I show you more appreciation for the lovely home you make for us. I propose that I give the kids more credit for being great teenagers, instead of fussing over little things."

Now it was the retreat group who brushed away tears as Kevin expressed his commitment again to Dena. He shared his desire to honor her in their marriage and concluded by saying, "I want you to know that I love you now more than I did thirty minutes ago."

The Agreement

Sometimes, as in Kevin and Dena's case, just one time through is enough to agree on a proposal. But sometimes after two or three times, the participants are still not ready to sign on the dotted line. At that point, the two of you may want to propose setting the issue aside for several days to think and pray about it, to seek godly counsel, or to gather more information before coming together for another session. Sometimes waiting a week or more is an acceptable course, depending on the issue and its urgency. Just be sure to set a time to reengage that suits you both.

Whenever agreement is reached, however, it is imperative to write it out, sign it and date it. Place it somewhere it can be referred to later. This is vital. Otherwise, a week later, two days later, or even two hours later, one is likely to say, "I'm so glad we agreed on X," only to be met by an adamant, "No, that's not what we said. We agreed to Y."

All your effort may be for naught if you don't write it down. Sometimes, the process of writing the agreement in black and white clarifies it and makes it more tangible. Writing it out makes it more concrete and helps us be specific and realistic. Having to sign helps both partners count the cost and affirm their commitment.

Remember, the decisions you make can be altered, but only if the two of you agree to change them at a later date. Sometimes it helps to try the proposal for a couple of weeks and see how it works. But do stay the course. Remain committed to your decision until you have an opportunity to walk the cross again about that issue.

Will it ever make sense to Dena that one or two dishes in the sink bother Kevin that much? It is unlikely. It may even seem bizarre to her. Does it make sense to him that she feels unappreciated when he notices one thing undone? Probably not. But both can say, "If it makes you feel this way, I can shift. I am willing to do things your way. While it doesn't make logical sense to me, I get it from an emotional point of view. Knowing how it affects you gives me a reason to change." If both are willing to shift perspective and habit, life is better. Freedom comes when we stop thinking about views as if they were right or wrong.

Gratitude always enhances pleasure. When Kevin comes home and notices that Dena has done what she promised, he can say, "Honey, thank you for having the kitchen so clean. It makes me happy." He knows it costs her time and effort to do it, and she deserves recognition. At the same time, he can overlook the occasional lapse and manage his own responses in a healthier way, staying emotionally connected and appreciative. Staying connected in the face of our differences is a great thing. We can feel satisfaction in learning to honor one another. Dena, in turn, finds it easier to defer to her husband's wishes because she better understands the emotional power her actions have on Kevin.

Neither is necessarily right, but each can enhance the relationship by making allowances for their differences.

Little Foxes

Kevin's problem with dirty dishes is probably tiny compared to issues you are facing in your own marriage. Truly, though, learning to negotiate little things successfully prepares us for larger ones. And even those little shifts can make life so much sweeter! Jesus says it this way, *"Whoever can be trusted with very little can also be trusted with much, and whoever is dishonest with very little will also be dishonest with much"* (Luke 16:10).

The Bible's Song of Solomon is a poetic look at the love relationship between a man and a woman. Notice this telling phrase, *"Catch for us the little foxes that spoil the vineyard"* (Song of Songs 2:15). Little annoyances breed discontent. And not uncommonly, minor things steal majorly the sweet fruit of a loving relationship. Like foxes scampering through a vineyard, little things may escape our notice. But if we don't look for them and catch them, they'll eat fruit and rob us of pleasure and joy. On the other hand, when we rid our vineyard of irritants, the harvest grows and is reaped in its fullness. By catching the "little foxes" that roam through the vineyard of our marriage, we experience more of the abundant life God desires for us.

If you are like me, you may wish to downplay little annoyances. "Oh, well, it's not that big of a deal; I hate to make an issue of it," I might tell myself. "Things are going pretty well. Why mess with a good thing?" This is the peacekeeping urge. Unattended, though, little things tend to add up and take away value. Over time, we may notice a lack of fruit —we're not having as much fun, and the relationship loses energy and passion.

As Kevin and Dena successfully catch that "little fox" of dishes in the sink, things go better for them. When either walks into the kitchen, the clean counter and sink are concrete reminders of the commitment they have made to honor one another. By deferring to Kevin's need, Dena is also empowered to speak up about things that she finds distressing. This is not from a mindset of keeping score, but from an attitude of openness and vulnerability. When one is empowered to ask for what s/he wants, the other can follow suit. In this, we practice freely giving and freely receiving. Our approach is always loving instead of legal. Needs and desires are not always logical. Nor are our feelings and perspectives. Yet they deserve an audience.

Even irrational irritations can be resolved by loving surrender. Coming to earth as a servant, Jesus leads the way. His kneeling before His followers to wash their feet was all wrong. They should have been bowing before Him. But in His actions and attitude, Jesus showed the depth and the breadth of His love (John 13:1-17). We can do that, too.

Every resolved issue infuses the system with a fresh burst of hope and confidence. With each resolution, a couple experiences the power of surrender and cooperation firsthand. Gradually, they forge an effective partnership and find the skills and the faith to tackle even the most troubling issues. It doesn't happen overnight, but it is well worth the persistent effort. Little by little, we find peace with each other and peace within. Peacemaking is worth whatever it costs!

Lean Into It!

When acquiring a new skill or working with a new tool, you can expect a bit of awkwardness at the beginning. Whether it is riding the bike or playing the piano, mastery is a process.

I remember learning to snow ski. My first day on the slopes was so miserable I nearly abandoned the effort. It was a gray day, with a bitingly cold wind. I felt frozen to the bone and my feet hurt. The snow-skiing gear and equipment felt bulky and awkward. And with too many things needing my attention, I fell more than once. The ride on the ski lift was especially unpleasant, and I missed my Texas heat. "People actually pay money to do this?" I asked myself as snow flurries assaulted the unprotected skin of my face.

I was unprepared for the experience. As a boy, I had many opportunities to water ski. I took to it quickly and I loved the feeling of jumping the wake on a slalom ski. I expected snow skiing to be easily mastered as well. I was wrong! Fortunately, my friend Gary encouraged me to hang in there. Plus, I had purchased a three-day lift ticket!

Remarkably, by day three I was "leaning in" to the experience. What had begun so uncomfortably became quite fun. While alpine skiing at first detracted from my love of the mountains, mastery of it eventually added a whole new thrill.

Of course I grew in competence over time. Now I love to use "snow blades" or "micro-skis" which make it easy to do 360's on the way down the slopes. Without poles, I feel more freedom and enjoyment, and traveling a little more slowly allows time to enjoy the snow-covered landscape. So if you are on the slopes of Colorado and see a goofy old guy singing and dancing his way down the mountainside, wave—it might be me!

Don't be discouraged if the process of *Take It to the Cross* feels awkward the first few times you use it. It takes time to learn and to "lean in" effectively. But if you start out slowly and give the tool an honest try, you'll make remarkable progress. Many couples are amazed at how smoothly the process goes, even the first time they try it. They find age-old problems melting away when approached in this manner.

Don't Forget to pray!

It is always good to start with prayer. Even when an issue is first brought up by either of you, it is a good idea to submit it to God from the start. When we turn His way and pray together, we recognize that neither of us has ultimate influence or control. Hearing one's mate verbally surrender to God in prayer helps undermine any sense of power struggle or manipulation.

It is certainly okay to ask God to change your partner's mind about an issue and even be bold in asking for exactly what you want, but remember to come back to the posture Jesus took in the Garden of Gethsemane when he added, *"yet not my will, but yours be done."* (Luke 22:42)

When you come together to walk the cross, it is a great idea to pray before beginning and perhaps also at the end. Jesus reassures us that if we seek God and His kingdom first, everything else will be fall into place. (Matthew 6:33)

In His final prayer with the apostles before going to the cross, Jesus prayed for unity. *"I have given them the glory that you gave me, that they may be one as we are one—I in them and you in me—so that they may be brought to complete unity. Then the world will know that you sent me and have loved them even as you have loved me."* (John 17:22,23).

This reveals the power of unity for us and for our impact in a dark world. Don't forget to pray!

You Can Do It

God is for you. He wants you to be unified. Conflict is not your enemy. On the contrary, avoidance of conflict is what robs relationships of power and intimacy. Having God rooting for your relationship is a comforting and empowering thought. He wants you to succeed!

As you put it to the test, this tool will help put an end to conflict avoidance in your relationship. As you practice, you will find yourselves addressing issues with open hearts and minds. After all, Jesus came to bring peace. Ephesians 2:14 declares, *"For he is himself our peace (our bond of unity and harmony). He has made us both, Jew and Gentile, one body, and has broken down (destroyed, abolished) the hostile dividing wall between us"* (*The Amplified Bible*. (1980). Grand Rapids, MI: Zondervan Bible.)

If He can do that for embittered cultures with centuries of animosity, He can do it for our marriages. He can break down the dividing wall of hostility and bring us to one mind. He is our peace.

TAKE IT TO THE CROSS

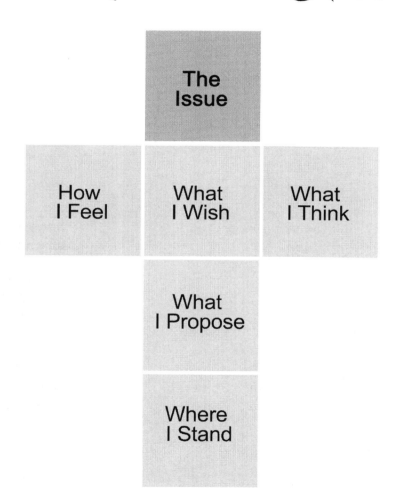

CHAPTER 4

THE ISSUE - NAME YOUR GAME

Consider Rob and Sara. They experienced ongoing tension about timeliness. Rob felt he was always waiting on Sara and felt frustrated when they were late for church or other events. To Sara, Rob's frustration seemed petty and controlling. Rob had, in fact, done everything he could think of to "help" Sara with her bad habit. Unfortunately, even special events were often colored by their mutual aggravation.

Most of us don't fight unless something is at stake. When we feel anger or irritation, it is often because the behavior of the other threatens us in some way or presents itself in opposition to our values and principles. Most conflicts erupt because they connect to deep issues.

When they took it to the *Cross*, Rob was able to spill out his deeper feelings to Sara. It helped him put words to his sense of powerlessness in relation to her and how tardiness made him feel embarrassed and weak. For him, walking in late signaled that his life was out of control, and he imagined others saw his late arrival as a lack of consideration. Plus, having no cushion of time increased his stress, leaving him feeling frustrated and irritable. In addition, his aggressive driving intensified when they were late and added more tension between them as he raced to make up time.

As he walked the *Cross*, Rob remembered the feeling he had when going on vacation as a child, waiting in the car while his father went to the office for a "few minutes" that wore on and on. He remembered feeling ashamed walking in late to Sunday school as a kid and how he hated having to wait for one student at school to finish his assignment before the entire class could go to recess. He had vowed he would not keep others waiting for him. Sara's lax attitude toward timeliness put him in conflict with this inner vow.

As she took her turn, Sara was able to let Rob know that she was sorry for causing him stress, but she also said it angered her when he pressured her about being on time. She did not share his level of concern about being late for events and even told him she thought it was okay to be "fashionably late." She realized she often procrastinated and frequently tried to put too many tasks in a limited time. Because she felt judged by Rob, she resisted what she perceived as efforts to control her. She rationalized that he was just being uptight about the whole business. Both of them were obviously feeling anger, so it was clear they needed to address the issue. The Bible warns that, *a hot-tempered person stirs up conflict, but the one who is patient calms a quarrel*" (Proverbs 15:18).

Like Rob and Sara, most couples experience intense feelings when conflicts arise. These clashes often revolve around common themes such as our needs for security, intimacy, and order, but they show up in day-to-day disagreements that often seem trivial on the surface. Nonetheless, addressing even small aggravations by taking them to the cross clarifies underlying relational dynamics so that power struggles can dissolve into peace.

Amazingly, one small positive change in the way we relate as a couple shifts everything in a positive direction. When the change comes from heartfelt agreement by both parties, it forges a sense of partnership and mutual respect and fosters an atmosphere of harmony. Plus, successful resolution of even the smallest disagreement generates hope. Hope is essential. Without it, marriages die.

By talking about a specific issue, like timeliness, Rob and Sara became mindful of the underlying dynamic of control and resistance. By becoming more aware of how their behavior affected each other, their hearts softened, and refreshed tenderness helped them focus more on feelings and less on facts.

Rob modified his approach with Sara so she felt less judged and pressured. He communicated how he was feeling, rather than trying to get her to agree he was right. On the other hand, she took pains to be more timely once she understood how tardiness affected him emotionally. After communicating their feelings, neither felt compelled to prove they were right about the issue.

Rob also found he could manage his anxiety and frustration better if he stayed focused on his own behavior. He proposed that he would go to the car several minutes before he actually wanted to leave, so Sara would not feel as if he were breathing down her neck. He hoped letting her know he was going to the car would provide a sense of urgency without pestering her. A couple minutes before needing to leave, he suggested he call on her cell phone to check in. If she knew then she was not going to be ready, she could let him know and apologize for being late. Both agreed that, if she was late, they would drive separately to events that had a starting time, such as church or a meeting.

This was hard for Rob, because he liked riding with Sara, but both agreed that riding separately was preferable to riding together in icy silence or hot debate. Rob and Sara knew that changing the dance would help interrupt their old pattern, which was clearly not ideal. And I had shared with them that any time we can change things up, it often get us out of gridlock.

Sure enough, they both demonstrated a shift in attitude and behavior. While they occasionally slipped back, their overall way of negotiating this age-old conflict changed for the better, and they both felt the benefit. Both moved from feeling victimized to being empowered.

Keep the Issue Simple and Clean

When bringing up an issue, check to see if your description of the issue betrays your bias. For Rob, naming the issue "timeliness to events" came across better than, "the issue is you always make us late!" In the same way, "disciplining the kids" is a better way to frame **The Issue** than "you always give in to the kids." "Managing our money" as an issue is preferable to, "the issue is that you are a tightwad." Try to keep the issue free of judgment. "Thanksgiving plans" is a better lead-in than "the issue is that we always spend Thanksgiving with your family."

Stick to Only One Issue!

Staying focused on one issue at a time requires discipline and dedication. Focusing in on a single aspect of life together is a skill every couple can learn. As proposed earlier, when either of you becomes aware of an issue, bring it to your partner's attention and ask to set a time to address it. When the time comes, make sure to stick with the issue at hand. If other issues come up, write them down for attention at another time.

Many couples find it helpful to address at least one issue a week using *Take It to the Cross*. This decision keeps communication flowing between the two and prevents slipping back into conflict avoidance mode or destructive fighting styles. With that in mind, keeping a list of issues is helpful.

Some issues are specific to a particular phase of life or only arise in a specific circumstance, while other issues are ongoing concerns. Of these, some can be resolved in a single session. Others, like finances and sexuality, are issues that evolve over time. We do well to converse about them even when we are happy about how things are going. The *Cross* provides a stimulus to reflect on the good feelings we have when things are working well, and helps us ride the wave of blessing. Even in the good times, though, talking about where we are helps us move on to the next level of satisfaction by defining our next positive actions.

For example, it is easier to take new ground sexually when things are already going well. Or with finances, a timely discussion when we are prospering allows us to exploit the blessings and maximize our investments and giving. We should not be ashamed to ask for more from God and each other as we grow together. He wants us to flourish and grow on every front. As stated in the beginning, *Take It to the Cross* is intended to help us grow even if we are not stuck. Why miss out on the opportunity to go from good to great?

At the end of the book, in Appendix One, you will find a list of topics that may serve as a guide for discussions that serve to foster a healthy and harmonious home.

This Is Really about That

As we saw with Rob and Sara, most issues tap into deep feelings and needs. The surface issues that arise may be manifesting ongoing tensions or old wounds. Couples fighting about money may actually be responding to feelings of betrayal or disrespect. They may be in a power struggle, challenging one another's loyalty or love, or feeling that security is being threatened.

With other couples, the core difficulty regarding finances may be divergent priorities or a conflict regarding materialism or tithing. If the content of the conversation is strictly on whether an item should be returned to the store, the deeper issue may be missed. The format of the *Cross* peels back the layers to expose those deeper things.

If we really want to enjoy life and each other, we must pay attention to the deep issues that truly matter. Whether our conflicts revolve around hobbies or habits, hygiene or house rules, God wants our hearts. The surface things we fight about will rarely matter in eternity, but the deeper issues may be of utmost importance. It helps when we remind ourselves that the conflicts we face are temporary. And while God is interested in everything we endure, He wants our focus to be on our character and investing in the lives of others. These things are eternal. Getting good at tapping into **How I Feel** will often bring deep and lasting concerns to the surface.

Seven Core Conflicts

In *The Seven Conflicts: Resolving the Most Common Disagreements in Marriage,* Tim and Joy Downs propose that virtually all the issues arising in marriage can be traced back to seven core needs. The seven basic concerns they see underlying conflict are security, loyalty, responsibility, caring, order, openness, and connection. (Downs, Tim, and Joy Downs. *The Seven Conflicts: Resolving the Most Common Disagreements in Marriage.* Chicago: Moody, 2003. Print.)

They propose that understanding these underlying issues helps us deal with the heart of the matter, not just symptoms. In Appendix Two is a summary of the seven conflicts taken from their excellent book. If you like, you may read it now or refer to it later to illuminate your core concerns. Either way, it provides a great way for you to identify and tune in to the deeper dynamics that fuel your craziest conversations.

Who Goes First?

Once the couple has agreed on an issue and the time and place to address it, each will be able to think deeply about the issue and to pray about it as well. Either party can also do a little research and check with others they respect to get input and perspective. It is sometimes helpful to ask other couples how they deal with the issue at hand. No need to "reinvent the wheel"!

When the time comes, each partner should be fairly clear about how much they care about the issue at hand and how much impact the decision will have on them personally. If the couple can determine who cares most, then that person should generally go first. If that is unclear, then whichever is feeling bolder or more courageous can take the floor. Obviously, walking the cross exposes us and we need courage to share authentically.

In the event that neither is clearly more invested or courageous, the toss of a coin is a perfectly acceptable way to decide who begins. And since God is at work in everything for good (Romans 8:28), this method may even let Him have a say in the matter. As noted, prayer is a good way to begin.

The partner who goes first gets to set the tone for the discussion of the issue and provide a context for thinking about it. Because they have skin in the game, their proposal may be already thought out and clearly articulated. And although they have not yet heard from the other mate, they can try to include the other spouse's needs and perspectives in their offered solution.

The starting partner may also anticipate and articulate some of the other partner's wishes views and feelings as they share, which can make the listener feel heard and understood even before s/he takes a turn. This greatly facilitates the process and gives the proposal more weight because it is clearly includes some of what is at stake for both parties.

If the same partner starts every time, be curious about the significance. It may say something about the relative emotional buy in of the two partners or how safe each feels expressing needs, thoughts and feelings. Sometimes it reflects on how empowered, desperate or hopeful each feels when it comes to engaging conflict. Don't rush to a conclusion, but do look into it. If you are the partner who tends to defer and let the other go first, shake it up. Challenge yourself to take the lead. This often allows a more proactive approach to problem solving, rather than reacting to what your partner shares.

TAKE IT TO THE CROSS

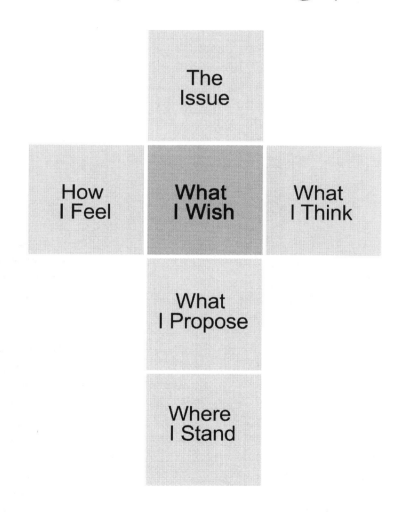

CHAPTER 5

WHAT I WISH—GET SMALL AND DREAM BIG

After defining **The Issue**, the person walking the *Cross* gets to share **What I Wish**. Telling what I wish forces me to think in ideal terms. It lets me dream big and share what life would be like if I had a magic wand and could make my world as I'd like it instantly. It also gives me an opportunity to say what I would wish for my partner.

Often, husbands' and wives' wishes are in sync, but reality impinges on our fantasies. For instance, if Teri and I are planning a vacation, an unlimited budget would be my fond wish, and Teri would heartily concur. Even so, I might imagine a tropical island destination, while Teri's magic wand would likely land us in Alaska or the Alps. When I say **What I Wish**, I can give words to what I wish for me as well as what I wish for her.

We bring to marriage a longing to be fully loved, accepted, and understood, and our big dreams fall hard. Even small areas of conflict trigger deep fears, powerful needs, and intense desires. The reality of life in a fallen world is most crushing in relationships with a large investment. The degree of our involvement and commitment drives the stakes enormously high. Like children, we often long for more than what is practical or even possible, but the longing reflects our desire for ideal love. And while dreams are valuable, communicating them as wishes shows we know they are often unrealistic or impossible. We all want "happily ever after," and voicing our dreams reminds both of us that we can't have everything we want. With effort, however, we can almost always move our relationship a little nearer our dream scenario.

Saying **What I Wish** puts words to our vision of the perfect world. Expressing ultimate desires in this way can be difficult and may feel like a huge risk, especially in the face of conflict. Truth is, many of us have trained ourselves to disqualify desires that seem unrealistic, unattainable, selfish, or silly. Voicing them, though, helps us be clear about what we truly desire, even if we can't have it. It is easier to relinquish something once we claim it, whereas unspoken desires may operate behind the scenes as expectations. We can't fully embrace and enjoy what we have until we grieve what we can't have.

Plus, voicing what I wish for myself and what I wish for my mate taps into my imagination and goodwill. Imagination, it turns out, is the opposite of judgment. Imagination fosters creative solutions and lets the sky be the limit, while judgment shuts down possibilities. Imagination allows us to be open and playful in contrast to judgment, which allows us the grim satisfaction of being right. Imagination seems risky because we have been dismissed for being unrealistic in the past, whereas judgment allows us to harden our hearts to disappointment because it tells us hope is not worth the risk.

Some of us learned this early on. We could not get what we wished for, so we squelched our desires. To dampen the pain, we told ourselves what we wanted was absurd. It helped the hurt, but at the expense of possibility. And many of us avoid disappointment by not asking for what we really want. In so doing so, though, we set ourselves up for regret, ending up with the disappointment we were determined to avoid.

As noted previously, a right/wrong mentality is deadly in conversations aimed at mutual understanding and resolution. For this reason, we need to step aside from judgment. Saying **What I Wish** moves my brain into an open and vulnerable mode, rather than staying closed and defended. It encourages me to dream and brings me back to a state of innocent desire. It engages a tender spot, inviting faith, hope, and love.

Authentic Self/Adaptive Self

When we were quite small, we were able to engage life honestly and naturally. We could be spontaneous and open, believing we were precious. We were at ease, fully assured that what we had to say or do was valuable and good. We lived in the moment and did not edit our speech. We were completely transparent. Like Adam and Eve in the garden before their disconnection from Life, we were naked and unashamed.

Regrettably, our true and innocent self falls under judgment. At some point, our own agenda comes in conflict with another's, and there is a clash. Unless we are able to use manipulation to obtain what we desire, we are forced to adapt. Even in the best of circumstances, we must surrender our authentic self to the demands of socialization. In worse scenarios, we are shamed for our appearance or behavior, or what we did was rejected as inadequate or bad. In all these moments, the authentic self is squelched, and the adaptive self makes its appearance.

This adaptive self is who we become to avoid the rejection our authentic self has received. It is the way we adapt to get along with others and minimize the risk of further pain in relationships. It includes our coping strategies and all the things we do to prove our worth. It shows up in our rationalizations and those internal compromises we make to avoid conflict. It includes all manner of maneuvering to avoid rejection, disdain, or further judgment. At its best, the adaptive self can produce strength and productivity, compliance and generosity, but it cripples and undermines our ability to be genuine and unguarded.

This is one reason this tool can be so helpful for us. Beginning with *What I Wish* and continuing with *How I Feel* and *What I Fear*, *What I Think* along with *What I Believe*, and *What I Need*, the process of *Take It to the Cross* invites us to engage our authentic self. Even *Where I Stand* allows us to connect profoundly with our deepest convictions and to proclaim them, clear and unwavering. Intimacy is not possible without authenticity.

Let Your Face Know!

One great advantage of standing and walking the cross is that it helps override our defensive and self-protective maneuvers. It helps us reveal our authentic self and we grow to be more tuned in to our feelings.

As we learn to be more transparent, our face can show our partner how we are feeling and how their behavior is affecting us. We feel compassion for little children when we see their displeasure. When they are sad, hurt, angry or disappointed, their little faces show it. They don't try to hide it and when they are very small, they don't even have the ability to cover up.

Sadly, when children are not given attention to and acceptance of strong emotions, they may learn to cover them up or shut them down. Some of us learned to harden our hearts and move into our heads. And when we did, we began to act out our feelings, rather than express them directly. As adults, we may launch them with criticism or blame, or go the other way and act overly nice. Those negative feelings may leak out in sarcasm or snide remarks or through griping and complaining. They may show up in passive behaviors or erupt in a violent display.

On the contrary, some children learn to use emotion to manipulate and control others. Through tears or tantrums, some kids are masterful at using strong emotions to to get what they want. They don't learn to squelch their feelings and so others end up being all too aware when they are unhappy. They struggle to be pleasant anytime their mood is disrupted, and still need to learn the value of courtesy and restraint. They must learn to modulate their feelings and tone them down so they can be shared truthfully, but lovingly, rather than harshly or manipulatively.

The message of grace is "Come as you are." When one we love shows on their countenance that they are sad or lonely, frustrated or repentant and give us appropriate words to go with it, we can express empathy. We can say, "I am sorry you are feeling that way. I care about you. Can I help?" Even anger expressed calmly can help us see clearly how our actions affect another. Solomon says it well, *"Better is open rebuke than hidden love."* (Proverbs 27:5)

At the end of the book, after the tear out sheets of the various steps of *Take It to the Cross*, there is a page naming various emotions. This can be used as a sort of "cheat sheet" for those who are challenged when it comes to emotional expression. Some of us may even need to stand in front of a mirror to practice facial expressions to reveal the state of our heart.

As a public speaker, I found it necessary to practice showing emotion and being more animated in order to effectively communicate my message. It felt awkward and forced at first, but as I practiced, I became more comfortable with being more demonstrative. Especially as my audience became more engaged, I was empowered to be even more expressive. If we want to connect with our partner, being expressive of emotion is vital.

At the same time, those who are naturally emotional may need to tone it down so their less expressive partner is not overwhelmed. For some people, emotional intensity feels unsafe and triggers a fight, flight or freeze response. For those like my wife, Teri, who were traumatized by a parent or sibling that gave full vent to feelings, strong emotional expression can easily feel overwhelming and scary.

Playfulness

Children are good at playing make-believe. This may be one reason Jesus asks us to become like them. Pride makes us feel we cannot afford to be playful or silly. Pride forces self-protection instead. Sharing fantasies or fears can make us feel vulnerable and small. Feeling small, silly, or weak may seem unsafe, but is the best invitation for warm and tender feelings from those who care about us. Even if those nearby judge us, being vulnerable offers the only real chance for deep connection with ourselves. Being authentic can feel really good, even when no one truly understands. This is especially true for those of us who have made a science out of revealing only what we think is realistic or acceptable.

As an example of **What I Wish,** when Teri and I talk about spending time together, I tell her I wish for her that we could be together twenty-four hours a day. At the same time, I wish for myself to have twelve hours a day for work, eight or nine hours a day for sleep, and about six for solitude, puttering, and reading. Obviously, what I wish for is not only unrealistic, it is impossible. However, it frames the conversation in a way that makes it clear neither of us can have just what we want. We realize that being in a fallen world and being in loving relationship both require death to self. Putting the conversation in context of **What I Wish** reminds us that we long for perfection, but can't really attain it.

Giving something to my mate in fantasy can feel very affirming, even if our wish for them is completely unattainable. Remember Dena and Kevin from chapter two? Dena felt great when Kevin wished he could give her a whole staff of servants.

And of course, great joy can be found by having a request granted that seems selfish. Sometimes I love being babied as Teri fulfills an infantile desire. Other times, acknowledging my immature or selfish longing makes letting go of it easier. I can grieve the loss of my ideal scenario and embrace a solution that meets the needs and desires of both of us, albeit imperfectly.

We can practice sharing our ideal scenarios with God. We can take even our most unrealistic wishes to God in prayer. He can give us clarity and peace about what would bring happiness to your relationship. Phillips Brooks states that, "A prayer in its simplest definition is merely a wish turned Godward." And in Ephesians 3:20, the apostle Paul encourages us about God's goodness and power, assuring us that He can do more than we ask or imagine!

A Word about Humor

Using humor as you engage conflict discharges a lot of tension and greatly diminishes the chance of an explosion. When sharing **What I Wish**, there is an excellent opportunity for hyperbole—stating things in grandiose or extreme terms. This often brings a smile and lightens the mood. Being witty or using puns as you walk the *Cross* can promote laughter and reduce anxiety and hostility.

Sarcasm, though, should be avoided like the plague. Sarcasm

uses positive words in a negative way. An example would be saying, "Oh, that was really smart," when the speaker actually infers that the action was stupid. The root words for sarcasm literal mean to "tear the flesh", and indeed sarcasm often conveys hostility and causes harm.

In contrast, irony can be appreciated. Saying to a brilliant spouse, "We know how intellectually challenged you are!" can be funny, especially when said in a good-natured way.

Playfulness, funny expressions, lighthearted kidding and innuendos can be advantageous when conversing about difficult things. Anything that brightens the mood can help as long as we are not seen as trying to minimize the importance of the conversation or the issue.

Of course, those of us who use humor as our default mechanism to avoid vulnerability may need to tone it down or avoid it completely during some discussions. We must learn other strategies to demonstrate vulnerability and emotional presence.

If we do not cross a line and go too far with humor, it can be very disarming. Self-deprecating humor can be particularly beneficial by conveying the message that we are not taking ourselves too seriously. When we laugh at ourselves, we take a step away from arrogance and pride, making ourselves smaller and more human. This too opens the door for connection.

TAKE IT TO THE CROSS

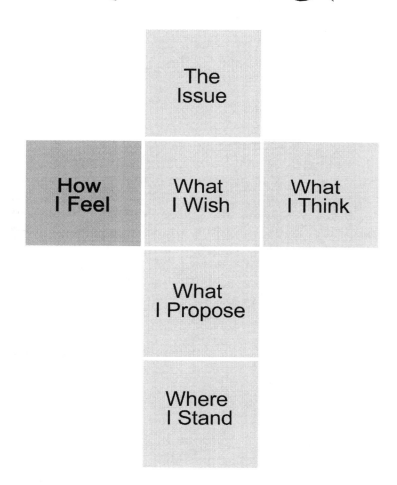

The
Issue

How
I Feel

What
I Wish

What
I Think

What
I Propose

Where
I Stand

CHAPTER 6

HOW I FEEL—EXPRESS FEELINGS TO REACH YOUR PARTNER'S HEART

Emotions alone do not make for good decisions, yet they must be honored. Sometimes emotions reveal the heart of the issue. They often give clues to reveal deep wounds, insecurities, needs, motives, and desires. Small children feel deeply. As adults, we can reclaim some of that childlike resilience and joy for life if we become better at accessing and expressing emotion.

At times, God's Spirit uses emotion to guide us. When God breathed into Adam's nostrils the breath of life, he made the body the repository of the spirit. The heart of a person resides in the chest, not in the skull. As such, breathing, heart rate, bodily tension, and sensation can all help us be aware of our own spirits and His Holy Spirit. To have life to the full, we must pay heed to what we feel.

One of the reasons I ask couples to walk the *Cross* rather than just sit and talk is that standing forces us to bear our own weight. In the upright posture, we can figuratively and literally take a stand for our own souls and for the relationship. It is striking for me to see how differently some people communicate while standing with the partner sitting attentively. For many, it brings a sense of responsibility and gravity to the conversation, while for others, the authentic sharing becomes more like a game and less threatening.

Apparently, we are more grounded when we stand—more alert, and better able to access feelings. Standing helps us express ourselves more clearly, and moving back and forth between thoughts and feelings helps us avoid becoming entrenched in our own position. It helps us step away from defensiveness or denial.

By being aware of feelings that arise in the body when addressing a particular issue, we learn to express both positive and negative emotions. This is like shining a light on our hearts, allowing us to unpack our feelings and reveal the emotional weight and significance of the problem for each partner. This is immensely helpful when it comes to making decisions.

On some issues, my emotional investment is tiny. For instance, it doesn't really matter much to me how the pantry is organized. But messy countertops can knock me into an emotional ditch. As we unpack our feelings around an issue, the intensity of our reactions reveals the power of the issue to move us. And as passions are revealed, we can find compassion for ourselves as we grasp the emotional burden we are bearing. In turn, we can readily access and offer compassion for our mate as they work to unravel their own heart's responses to the matter.

Because men tend to be won over by appeals to logic, we often try to keep emotions out of decision-making. But the impact of an issue on the heart of her husband carries more significance and is more appealing to a woman than his rational dissertation. This proves true especially when she feels bullied by facts or feels approached as if his way is the "right way." Since they tend to be more relational, women are more likely to shift perspective when they see the emotional impact of a decision on one they love. While it may seem offensive to override logic with love, scripture assures us that *"mercy triumphs over judgment"*

(James 2:13).

As a matter of fact, individuals with injury to the part of the brain that processes emotion—the ventromedial prefrontal cortex—tend to make bad decisions or struggle to make any decision at all. <u>We need emotion to move us in the right direction!</u>

How I Feel is an invitation to get out of my head and into my heart. It helps me get real by authentically sharing my inner experience. Because conflict stirs deep emotions, this arm of the *Cross* helps me tap into core issues that may reveal as never before the power my partner has to lift me high or to push me toward the pit.

When we are moved by another's behavior, it makes sense to <u>acknowledge it to ourselves and then share it</u> with the other. If we don't, we are likely to focus on their behavior and provoke defensiveness or shame. If we don't share the emotional impact of our mate's actions and instead focus on the offending behavior, our mate will likely be overrun by their own distress at being exposed and potentially judged. Thus, they miss the chance to feel compassion for us in our distress.

The apostle Paul encourages us to think in loving terms rather than legal. In 1 Corinthians 6:12 he says that everything is lawful, but not everything is helpful. Many of the things that bother me about Teri, or Teri about me, are things that are not objectively wrong. They just happen to be things that feel unloving, inconsiderate or disrespectful. When we share our feelings about them, we are in a much better mode than when we try to convince each other we are right.

The question is, will we expose our mate or ourselves? Will I acknowledge my own shame at being so vulnerable, or will I launch it onto them? Of course it is difficult, because I feel like a baby when I am so sensitive to Teri's behavior. I confess I feel defective if I am not strong, impervious, or resilient in the face of her neglect, betrayal, disapproval, or inconsideration. Through practice, though, I am learning to embrace the beauty of connection and the way it makes us like little children.

As I learn to honor my own feelings, then I can also honor my wife by sharing authentically. However, when anger is the dominant emotion, I often need to process it and get to deeper and more tender feelings in order to avoid doing harm. Once again, the effort is worth it.

Learn to Speak Emotion

We must develop the skill to access our emotions. Some of us had parents who pressed in, encouraging us to find words to express emotions rather than act them out. They taught us, "Use your words." These parents validated our deep feelings and authorized their expression. If they saw us in distress, they encouraged us to open up about our feelings. Sometimes they guessed at them and asked for confirmation. "You look sad. Are you okay?" "I bet you feel angry now." "Are you disappointed you didn't get a part in the play?" "You must feel happy that you worked so hard on your spelling words." They sat with us in our grief and reveled in our delight. Even when we were full of anger or frustration, healthy parents encouraged us to talk our feelings out and work them through.

Others of us were not so fortunate. Our moms and dads were uncomfortable with strong emotion, or maybe our parents were simply preoccupied and unavailable. Many of our parents sent myriad messages that our feelings were wrong or that we should not express emotions. "Children are to be seen and not heard!" Whether we were too boisterous or bawling, we were told to tone it down. Sometimes we were shamed for tender feelings. "Don't be a crybaby!" "Go to your room until you can put on a happy face!" We learned to squelch emotion or to avoid it altogether. Sometimes we were even told, "That's not really how you feel!"

I grew up in a home where I was shamed for being sensitive and the expression of angry emotions was met with hostility or punishment. I was also shamed when I asked for help. Even in college, I was still so disconnected from my feelings that I didn't even know what made me angry.

For those of us not naturally good at voicing our feelings, this arm of the *Cross* takes practice. Even seemingly small emotions, like irritation, can be big factors when addressing conflict. Ongoing irritations rob us of joy. As noted before, the little foxes often spoil the vineyard, and acknowledging mild emotions can help us tap into deeper and more powerful feelings. Because emotional and spiritual connections develop in the heart, accessing emotion can help us connect with God and our mates more deeply and fully.

From research and personal experience, we know we can't suppress negative emotions without dampening the positive ones as well. Unexpressed negative emotions can block the flow of powerful emotional expressions. We must clear away the negative feelings so we can enjoy the positive. Like digging for buried treasure, we find the heart of gold only after digging through the dirt. As we listen to our hearts, we can also get better at tuning in to the voice of God in our soul's inner rooms.

Love, joy and peace are the first fruits of the Spirit listed in Galatians 5:22-23. If you think about it, all of these influence and flow through our emotional self. As we grow in loving as God loves, we will experience more peace and more joy. And more peace and joy making loving and being loved easier and more natural. Even God responds to good and evil by feeling love or hatred. He loves righteousness and hates evil, rather than being motivated by a legal posture of reward and punishment. Mercy, tenderness, compassion, and anger are ascribed to Him throughout scripture. Having emotion is part of what it means to be made in His likeness. Our emotional experience is extremely important to God, so it honors Him when take time to feel and deal with emotion.

Dig Deep!

If we want to tap in to the power of emotion and the life of the Spirit, journaling is our portal. It awakens us to our inner world, allowing us to identify what is at work in our hearts where God resides. As a daily practice, it keeps us open and curious regarding our experiences—how they move us, and what they teach us. Even journaling only sporadically will still heighten self-understanding and help us grow.

If we journal in our worst moments, we can catch and release the negative emotions that can rob us of peace and joy. As we thoughtfully journal our moments of enlightenment, we can capture and hold on to the lessons we learn. If life is a journey, capturing in words what we see from the mountaintops and what we find in the valleys will equip us to live lives of meaning and fulfillment and arrive at a good destination. Our written words help us learn our lessons well and prevents our having to learn them repeatedly.

Journaling is a way of self-reflecting. Just as seeing emotion mirrored in the face of a parent validates the child's emotions and helps the youngster connect with what she is feeling, writing our feelings validates their significance. It reveals the value we place on our own souls, just as the Psalms did for David. In Psalms 22 and 35, he refers to his own "precious life." Articulating our experience in black and white invites us to take ownership of our emotions and to wrestle with what they mean for us and how we wish to respond to them. We feel calmer and more in control of emotions when we write them out. If we avoid feeling and dealing with emotions, they are apt to hijack and control us in ways we may not appreciate.

For these reasons, I am a strong advocate for journaling. Men, even more than women, may require solitude to process emotions, since women are good at processing through conversation. After processing alone, I find my clients can more easily articulate their experiences when we meet. Journaling is equally valuable in marriage, enabling us to go deeper and to share more fully with our mate. It makes much more sense to ask for an audience with my spouse when I have taken the time to listen thoroughly to the cry of my own soul.

Feel to Heal

When talking from *How I Feel*, try to anchor every statement in a feeling. Difficult issues often make negative emotions appear more dominant and might even mask some of the positive feelings you may have about the topic at hand. For this reason, be deliberate about investigating your heart on the topic, and share both the negative and positive feelings. Ask yourself, "Am I happy we are discussing this? Am I hopeful or discouraged about this issue? Do I feel grateful for how far we have already come? Am I excited about the possibilities or am I fearful that we will remain stuck? Does this issue lead to feelings of frustration or anger? Do

I feel hurt or sad about it? Do I have any regret, shame, or embarrassment regarding the topic? Do I feel sorry for the way I have handled this issue in the past? Do I feel alone in dealing with the issue, and has it led to feelings of isolation, betrayal or abandonment? How do I want to feel about this issue?"

It is especially important to share your negative views from *How I Feel.* Sharing them in this way takes ownership of them and lets your partner know just how much distress you are feeling. Since we process negative feelings in the limbic system deep in the right hemisphere of our brain, I always place the *How I Feel* card as the right arm of the cross. We all know that our perspectives can be distorted and that our feelings are sometimes way more powerful and negative than we might wish. Sharing them is important, and it may help our partner hear them if we qualify them—"In my worst moments, I feel . . ."

Especially when you are making a negative observation about your partner, it is much better to share it from "I feel" than "I think." If I say to Teri, "It *feels* as if you always do what is important to you, but you forget about me," I reveal my hurt. But if I say, "I *think* you always do what is important to you, but you forget about me" she is more likely to take offense. In that case, she will appeal to her own truth and want to set me straight.

Sharing my perception as a thought will often come across as a judgment, and judgment provokes defense. She can argue with my thoughts, but my feelings belong to me. I may be wrong about my feelings, but I have a right to them. Sharing a negative *thought* invites rebuttal. Sharing a negative *feeling* more effectively invites understanding, reassurance, or comfort.

Unacknowledged feelings can fuel a desire to prove we are right. If we are uncomfortable with emotional vulnerability, we tend to judge our tender feelings as irrelevant or weak. Judging our own deeply personal reactions to life, we are set up to pass judgment on those close to us as well.

Especially delicate or fragile revelations may provoke the same response we give ourselves. "Suck it up!" "It's not that big a deal!" "You are way too sensitive!" We build a case for our position and impose our view on others. While this strategy is rarely effective, we console ourselves with the belief that we are right.

Self-righteousness is a tasty morsel we can eat even when everyone else is held at arm's length. It can keep us going and numb us to the pain of alienation from others and from our own souls.

Remember, you don't have to be right about your feelings to have a right to your feelings!

Deep, Dark Dread

While sharing feelings, it is helpful to ask yourself, "What is it that I fear?" Revealing **What I Fear** is a gift. It clarifies what is at stake for my mate and me in our difficult conversations. Addressing our deep fears helps uncover underlying motives, allowing us a chance to shift and step away from fear. When we see our mate's anxieties, it can rekindle tenderness, activate compassion, and promote unity.

As an example, I may realize my big fear is being told I am selfish or that I am being a baby. Since I heard those words spoken in harshness and judgment when I was a boy, being viewed in that light as an adult seems intolerable. It makes me feel small and despised.

To avoid feeling needy, I determined to always put others' needs first. After being shamed for my desires and told they were selfish and immature, I got really good at squelching them. Even now, I resist feeling and sharing my wishes and needs, fearing I will get judgment and rejection in return. But I have found that speaking my fears aloud makes them less scary. I can see they are irrational, and sharing helps my partner respond with tenderness and compassion.

Expressing irrational fears and selfish desires is not only permissible, it is an important part of negotiating with my mate. Being a baby is okay, as long as we take turns being weak or strong for one another. What devastated us in the past does not have to control us now.

It can be scary to look under the bed and acknowledge our fears, but shining a light on dark places in our souls illuminates them and helps us see that the monster under the bed has only as much power as we give it. Things that haunted us previously can be overcome. They lose their power as we acknowledge them and view them in the light.

Naturally, if we are completely unguarded in relationship we must be willing to suffer the pain of misunderstanding, rejection, or judgment. Ironically, willingness to risk these things makes them less likely to occur. When we defend ourselves against misunderstanding, rejection, or judgment by refusing to be vulnerable, we are most likely to find ourselves judged, misunderstood, and rejected.

When I tell Teri, for instance, how wrong she is for failing to check in with me or pick up her phone when she is out with friends, I am confronting her about what I see as bad behavior. This is a shaming approach that makes me feel justified in my anger. When I point out that I don't do that to her, I further justify my position. Obviously, it feels safer to express anger than the more vulnerable feelings of insecurity and hurt. Accusations and justifications can be launched in anger from my self-protective fortress. But putting down my guard and taking an honest look at how I feel when she is unavailable to me can be much more powerful.

"It bothers me when are out with friends and I don't hear from you. Particularly if I call and you don't pick up, I feel unimportant and neglected. That makes me feel sad and disconnected. Sometimes I am afraid I'm not even on your radar if you don't have a need for me.

"When you are gone longer than you planned and don't check in, I start feeling anxious. Sometimes I imagine the worst. I know it doesn't make sense, but it makes me feel loved when I hear from you and when you are accessible.

"I know how difficult it is to hear your phone when you are in a noisy place, so it means a lot when you make an effort to keep your phone where you can hear it."

Of course, being vulnerable makes me feel like a baby and sometimes I sound like one. Ironically, in the intimate connection of marriage, we can be exquisitely sensitive to our partner's attentions or lack thereof. Being rejected, unappreciated, or unacknowledged can feel devastating even when we know rationally that the slight was completely unintended. High emotional investment heightens our responsiveness to one another.

For a wonderful picture of a child's sensitivity to attunement with mom, watch the video entitled "The Still Face Experiment" with Dr. Ed Tronick. (https://youtube/apzXGEbZht0) When the mother stops tuning in to her child, the child almost immediately feels distressed. Without yelling or even mildly scowling, the lack of response to the child is almost unbearable.

And although we are not infants, our susceptibility to our partner's lack of availability can be deeply distressing. We may not show it, but an absence of attention, affection, or affirmation in marriage can feel horrible, not unlike the way the way the infant in the video experiences her mother's lack of response. Of course, over time even babies shut down on their needs if consistently neglected. We must be deliberate in accessing and expressing vulnerable needs and feelings or we put ourselves at risk for ceasing to care.

The enemy of our souls knows that trusting enough to be vulnerable is what opens the way for connection, so he constantly whispers words that undermine trust and intimacy. "She doesn't care." "He won't protect you." "She won't understand." "He'll never change." Satan knows he has the upper hand if he can introduce doubt and fear about the other person's motive. This was his tactic with Eve in the garden. Even though God was extremely generous with Adam and Eve and only withheld what He knew would hurt them, the serpent found a way to make God seem unreasonable.

If he can make God look bad, imagine how easy it is for the enemy to convince my wife to doubt my love for her or to question her affection for me. He made Eve doubt God and left her thinking she couldn't trust her Father to tell her the truth, so she didn't go to Him. Instead, her uncertainty prompted her to resolve the conflict on her own. But unilateral decisions in loving relationships almost always undermine unity and, as Adam and Eve found, can end very badly.

Take Up Your Cross

Sharing **What I Fear** is an act of courage and trust. It paints a picture of my worst-case scenario. If I do a good job of baring my soul, it is probably an extreme outcome that I fear and probably unrealistically negative, even as **What I Wish** is unrealistically positive. Sharing my deep fear can steer the conversation away from those worst outcomes and give my partner a chance to reassure me that she is not my enemy.

These wishes and fears bring into focus both bright and dark spots in our hearts, reminding us how we can soar or plummet in the face of almost any issue. While remaining strictly rational may seem like a good idea, it doesn't promote understanding or grace. Sounding out deeply held desires and dread, on the other hand, help us navigate the waters of conflict without sinking our ship. Identifying these submerged emotions allows us to have safe passage through the rough waters of difficult conversations. Desires propel us along in our journey toward ideal understanding and harmony, while voicing fears helps us avoid destructive setbacks.

No matter how clear we are about our goals, or how strong we think we are, we ignore wishes, fears, and feelings at our own peril. As those aboard the Titanic found, scraping up against something submerged and unseen can not only interrupt our progress, it can take us under.

Obviously, it takes maturity and strength to risk revealing our immaturity and weakness. We must be more committed to self-revelation than self-protection. This is the message of the incarnation—Jesus' becoming human. The Son came to show us that our Father God is more committed to revealing Himself than protecting Himself. The cross is the demonstration that God will be hung out to die before He will retreat from engagement with us. When we *Take It to the Cross* we take on the same attitude.

So, although they make us feel vulnerable, give feelings their due. Many of us tend to avoid them, but they can make all the difference in how we resolve our issues. And even when they don't provide resolution to our problem, airing them clears away resistance and fosters intimacy.

I'll say it again: finding a solution to your problem is not as big a win as connecting heart-to-heart. Remember—conflict can be our point of connection. Practice sharing **How I Feel** and **What I Fear**.

TAKE IT TO THE CROSS

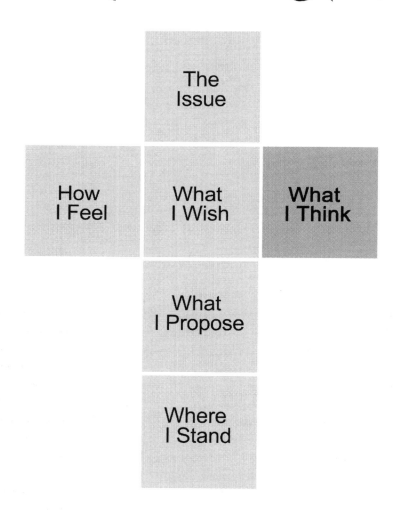

The
Issue

How
I Feel

What
I Wish

What
I Think

What
I Propose

Where
I Stand

CHAPTER 7

WHAT I THINK- USE REASON AND FAITH TO OFFER THE BENEFIT OF THE DOUBT

Even as emotions are part of good decision-making, so too research, reason, and faith help us identify good solutions. After expressing emotion, our minds can step back from the immediacy of feelings and make observations to inform and clarify the facts. This is probably because our emotional self is more central in our brain and led by our survival drives. If we don't pay attention to feelings, they have us in their grip. Before we uncover and express feelings, fears, and desires, our reasoning power can be used to rationalize what we want. But when we express those emotions and wishes, we can more easily set them aside. Released from the grip of fear and feelings, the mind does a better job processing rationally and hopefully.

When stepping to **What I Think**, the speaker attempts to give an objective and fair-minded view of the situation at hand. While our subjective and emotional view from **How I Feel** may be dark at times, our thoughts, ideas and perspectives shared from **What I**

Think can shed light on any issue. Here too is where we share *What I Believe* to be true.

As noted previously, negative feelings are processed on the right side of our brain. The left brain is more logical and is the seat of language. It is where we experience more positive emotions. So after expressing the dark side on *How I Feel* we can step left to *What I Think* and give a brighter, more hopeful view. Always think, "Left means language, logic, and light." When we step left, we step into the light of objective and rational ideas, beliefs, thoughts, and hopes. This is also where we bring in research and the power of reason.

Here's an example: When life gets hectic for Teri and me and we address the issue of spending time together, my wife might tap into *How I Feel* saying, "I feel like I never see you. It seems I get the leftovers of your day, and sometimes it feels like you don't even want to spend time with me." That stings!

Everything in me wants to jump in, superimposing my view of reality. I want to bust in with, "Are you kidding me?" But if I hold onto my urges and wait, she will almost always move on to *What I Think* about the issue and share a different view. "I know you love me and we did have a great night out on Tuesday. When we went away for the weekend, everything seemed better. I think you do a good job of balancing all your activities. Still," she says, stepping back to *How I Feel*, "I have a strong desire for more quality time with you. I need you!" And moving left again, she may add, "What I believe is that we can be more intentional about our times together."

As is obvious from this example, all of us are capable of having a dim view as well as a brighter perspective on any topic. If we engage the process fully, we will do our best to share both. Some of us need to get out of heads into our hearts, while others of us desperately need to be freed from the tyranny of our emotions.

A "heart person" will often marry a "head person." It is far better to achieve balance by moving toward one another, rather than engaging in a figurative tug-of-war, in which each tries to pull the other to their side of the conflict. In this case, the heart person can learn to make a more reasoned appeal, while the head person learns to speak feelings.

It often helps to examine an issue from the other's point of view. In doing so, we learn to give the benefit of the doubt when interpreting our partner's behavior. While *How I Feel* may bring the worst-case scenario into view, disciplined exploration of *What I Think* can almost always help me imagine a better possibility and believe for the best.

Be on guard against using brainpower to rationalize. Rationalizing is an attempt to explain or justify behaviors or attitudes with logical, plausible reasons, even if these are not true or appropriate. Rationalizing seeks to justify or excuse us. It is a form of defensiveness, and it gets in the way of true connection. Where rationalization exempts us from responsibility by seeking justification for our actions, reason helps us engage obstacles in a positive and creative way.

Watch out for using your mind to defend the status quo. "That's just the way I am," can stand in the way of growth and transformation. Rationalization generally lets us off the hook, in contrast to reason, which uses brainpower to engage problems in a responsible way.

Healthy partnerships cultivate the attitude that both are on the same team. While we know there is an enemy of our souls, our mate is not that enemy! *What I Think* provides the stimulus for articulating our more hopeful, generous, and faithful perspectives.

When we try to give each other the benefit of the doubt, we can usually identify a more positive motivation for our partner's behavior than the one Satan tries to highlight in our minds. He is masterful at this, and unhealthy partners listen to his spin on the relationship. With Eve, he successfully planted doubt in her mind about God's goodwill. You can rest assured it is still a favorite tactic for him to use on us. And he is very subtle.

The master of deception—delights in putting a spin on the truth. He is expert in activating the suspicion that our partner is not there for us. If he can turn that doubt into a judgment, so much the better. Judgment is "case closed" on communication. Unfortunately, when you have known someone a long time with all his or her weaknesses and flaws, judgment comes easy. Sometimes we even pride ourselves in predicting our partner's negative behavior. "He'll never go for that!" "I knew she would say that!"

Setting aside judgment is extremely tough, because judgments protect us. As they accumulate, they harden our hearts and leave us less vulnerable to hurt and disappointment. "I knew you would forget!" reveals a negative expectation, steeling me against disappointment and giving the grim satisfaction of being right.

What I Would Like to Think—Giving the Benefit of the Doubt

The remedy for judgment is to give your partner the benefit of the doubt. We do well to ascribe the best possible motive to our mate. Couples who practice this bring out the best in one another. We all, consciously or unconsciously, respond to the expectations of others for better or for worse. When we are seen in a negative light, overcoming the bias of another is difficult indeed. On the other hand, when we hear our partner express the hope that we are truly committed to their well-being, we feel a desire to activate our best self in line with that positive view. Giving the benefit of the doubt goes a long way toward increasing goodwill in our relationship. Love always takes the high road. *"Love is patient, love is kind... it keeps no record of wrongs...It always protects, always trusts, always hopes, always perseveres"* (1 Corinthians 13:4-7).

Putting this passage into practice is hard work. It takes energy to rise above our temptations to judge and self-protect. Like water, our thoughts flow downhill unless we deliberately lift them higher. The second law of thermodynamics in physics is often called the law of entropy. In simple terms, it states that a closed system runs down. Without a source of energy from outside, any system goes from high to low energy and from order to chaos. Our minds and our marriages seem to bear this out. Without attention and effort, human thoughts drift toward negativity and relationships lose their vitality.

If we want to keep a positive view of our mate and our marriage, we must choose to focus on the positive. Viewing our mate as a manifestation of Christ's presence in our lives makes it easier. In this way, we can do with them what God chooses to do for all of us. He imputes all of Jesus' great qualities to us, seeing us as He sees His own dear Son. When we are willing, He gives us grace to see our mate in the best possible light. Ask Him. He will help you!

At the very least, when we feel despair or express negative views of our marriage and mate, we can follow up with a desire to be proven wrong. "Sometimes I think you will always regret that I got pregnant and we 'had to' get married. I hope I am wrong." "You don't seem to care if we ever have sex again. I want to be wrong!"

Thinking Beyond the Problem to the Source

Sometimes **What I Think** gives opportunity to reflect on what lies behind our divergent views. Ask yourself, "Does this issue bring back echoes from the past?" Curiosity and exploration are key attributes in promoting understanding. Does the intensity of my reaction reveal that I have some unfinished business from childhood or a prior relationship? Does my partner's attitude, tone of voice, or behavior put me back into a painful chapter from the past? Be willing to take a look. Openness, acceptance, and curiosity oust judgment.

It can be immensely helpful to offer a context for your strong reactions. For example, it helps my wife for me to share that her forgetfulness recalls my childhood experience of neglect. She knows that being the third of four children whose parents worked and went to graduate school left me feeling that no one really saw me or felt my needs. When she gets distracted or overrun by obligations, forgetting what I have asked makes me feel everyone else's needs are more important than mine. I can easily slip into feeling that she just doesn't care. And when I get into those old feelings, I tend to respond in childish ways.

When I feel I am not on her radar, I can go into a deep funk almost instantly. My reaction can be way beyond what the immediate circumstance dictates, and I become prone to over-interpreting her actions. Not only that, but my brain begins to dredge up other examples of her lack of attention to me as I tell myself how I would never do that to her.

This happened recently when I misunderstood a text she sent and believed she was headed home without going a few blocks out of her way to touch base with me. Although I felt much better when she did come by later, I could have spared myself some grief by owning my part in it and giving her the benefit of the doubt.

Get good at exploring thoughts about your issues. This will help you take advantage of all you have learned from the past as a couple. Sometimes simply stating that we have been down this road before helps both partners remember that God got us through then and He can do it again.

When saying **What I Think**, be sure that you continue to use "I" statements. Sharing thoughts as judgments will block receptivity. An example of this would be stating, "I think you are oblivious to my needs." Another example would be the assertion, "It's obvious your boss wants to get into your pants. And I think you like the attention." It also comes across as a judgment if you make statements that come across in a condescending way. "Making a budget is not rocket science." "Anyone can see that what you are doing is irrational."

If you have done some research on the issue you are facing or talked it over with someone who has credibility, please feel free to share it with your partner. Just be sure you take ownership of what you think based on what you have learned, rather than using the authority to prove you are right. When I work with a couple in counseling, I caution them against using, "Dr. Looney says...!" as a way to gain leverage for one's position.

Along with **What I Think**, you can venture deeper by sharing what you hope for and **What I Believe**. Even when the rational mind sees a dead end, the eyes of faith may see possibility. Abraham, our father in the faith, shows us how to hold on to faith in the face of rational despair. He had waited many long years wishing and waiting for a child. Finally, at eighty-two, God promised it would happen. Even then, it was another seventeen years for the promise to be fulfilled. Sometimes we get tired of hoping and holding out for change. Because we have lived with things one way in our marriage for many years, it becomes difficult to believe they could ever be different. But if we take a tip from Abraham, we have hope.

He is our father in the sight of God, in whom he believed—the God who gives life to the dead and calls into being things that were not.

Against all hope, Abraham in hope believed and so became the father of many nations, just as it had been said to him, "So shall your offspring be." Without weakening in his faith, he faced the fact that his body was as good as dead—since he was about a hundred years old—and that Sarah's womb was also dead. Yet he did not waver through unbelief regarding the promise of God, but was strengthened in his faith and gave glory to God, being fully persuaded that God had power to do what he had promised.   - Romans 4:17-21

Can we have that same confidence? Ask God to give you hope and a vision for life as He would have it. Declaring positively **What I Think** and **What I Believe** when looking through the eyes of faith can empower us to change how we do business as a couple. After all, *"this is the victory that has overcome the world, even our faith"* (1 John 5:4).

Henry Ford said it well—"Whether you think you can or you think you can't, you're right." What we believe affects our reality and opens or limits our possibilities. Jesus affirmed repeatedly, *"According to your faith let it be done to you"* (Matthew 9:29). Do you have faith for your marriage? If so, declare it! If not, ask for it!

It is always good to hear words of encouragement and hope come from your own mouth or from another. Especially when we feel discouraged and hopeless about an issue, speaking faith and hope into a situation is extremely powerful. We have reason for hope. God is with us and wants to help us move ahead with strength and tenderness.

Even if we have been entrenched in a power struggle, God is able to show us a new way. In fact, if God has His way, we will all grow and be changed. Of course, with us God doesn't always get His way, but when we look to Him, there is reason for hope. While sharing **What I Think**, don't miss out on a chance to declare what you hope for and **What I Believe**.

TAKE IT TO THE CROSS

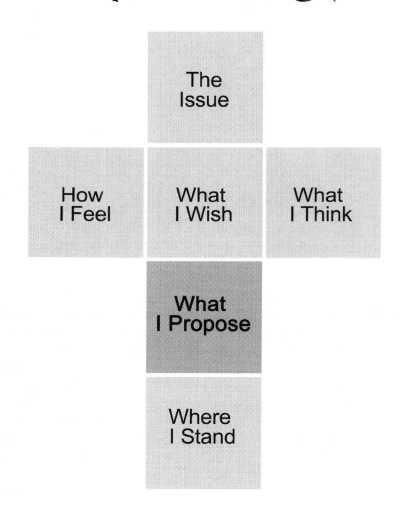

The
Issue

How
I Feel

What
I Wish

What
I Think

What
I Propose

Where
I Stand

CHAPTER 8

WHAT I PROPOSE–BRAIN STORMS TO SUNNY SKIES

In many marriages, the only end to conflict is giving up, giving in, or getting your way. But *Take It to the Cross* allows a win–win conversation, fostering confidence that with practice and help we can find a workable solution to any issue. If we apply ourselves and ask God's help, we can arrive at a decision both of us can endorse as good.

At the proposal step, we may toss into the arena every possible remedy, including those that are impractical or even sound ridiculous. Some ideas that seem outlandish at first glance are ultimately do-able and satisfying. Don't be afraid to dream big or think outside the box. Later on, you can take a stab at formulating a proposal that honors the perspectives and priorities of both husband and wife. Eventually, we can craft a proposal that is concrete and practical.

As an example, a couple addressing the use of sketchy language in the home will benefit by something more than "I propose we all get better at catching ourselves when we say a bad word." A helpful proposal is one that gives some traction with a concrete mechanism for addressing slips of the tongue when they occur. Designing and implementing a system with consequences takes energy, but will likely give a better result. A worthy proposal might sound something like, "I propose we get a piggy bank and fine the kids a quarter whenever they use a word on our bad list. You and I can contribute a dollar any time we slip up. We can make a game of it and use the money for family night. When we collect enough money, we can go out to a movie instead of watching one at home."

By making a game of it, everyone is more likely to get on board to help curb a bad habit. Of course, if a proposal will affect your children, it is powerful to include them in the process, too. Sometimes they will come up with the most creative and effective solutions. Children tend to love the opportunity to speak into an issue that affects them. And participating in the process enhances buy-in. Using the *Cross*, young ones can learn early how to negotiate and honor others' needs and perspectives.

Recently, a couple taught their teenage son *Take It to the Cross* to address a serious concern with his school performance. Imagine their surprise when he asked the next week to use the *Cross* with them to address a completely separate issue! He felt empowered by the process and valued the structure that helped him be heard without interruption.

When used for family decisions, of course, each person who takes the floor will begin by summarizing what the prior family member has shared. If only one child is involved in the discussion, it may work better for one parent to speak for both mom and dad so the process is simpler and doesn't feel like two against one. I often recommend that Mom take the lead with parenting younger children and Dad take the lead role as children move toward adolescence. A good rule of thumb is to make the shift at about age twelve for girls and fourteen for boys. Moms often do best at nurturing, while dads often excel at launching.

Proposals should be as concrete and measurable as possible. If the issue is saving for the children's education, for instance, each partner ought to think deeply about strategies for saving, clarifying time frames and mechanisms for feedback. It is almost always a good idea to add accountability to others, such as a financial planner or prayer partner.

The proposal does not have to be the final answer to a problem. It does, however, need to move us farther down the path toward resolution. If the issue is deciding on a church home, coming up with a schedule to visit a few churches may be an excellent proposal to get us moving in the right direction.

No Immediately Clear Path?

What if you can't readily agree a common proposal? This does not mean resolution is impossible or that you have wasted your time. When it happens, I strongly urge that you conclude your discussion with a prayer for clarity and calm. Both parties can commit to more thought and prayer for finding a way forward, and agree on a date and time to come back together. As mentioned earlier, the Holy Spirit can use the time to enlighten us and awaken in us a deeper understanding and compassion for our mate. This gap in time can assist both parties in being open to yielding and compromise. We can gather more information and seek good counsel as well.

Write It Down!

Several passes through the process may be necessary to reach resolution. The idea is to come up with a proposal that leaves both partners feeling good. In fact, what we wish for is a resolution that both can heartily endorse. Stephen Covey asserts that any answer two or more people can agree on is a better solution to a problem than anything any one of them could arrive at independently. (Covey, Stephen R. *The Seven Habits of Highly Effective People: Restoring the Character Ethic.* New York: Simon and Schuster, 1989. Print.) This is often true in practical terms, but it is always true in relational terms because peaceful agreement is a huge win for relationships.

After deciding on a proposal, it must be written, dated and signed. This prevents forgetting or unconscious editing later. Plus, writing it heightens the level of clarity and commitment.

And actually signing our names helps to seal the deal. Posting it somewhere reminds us of our joint decision and fosters accountability. Setting a standard of intent and behavior activates our consciences and heightens our awareness of how we relate. If the issue is ongoing, we can revisit the written agreement from time to time and review our success in the endeavor, making adjustments as needed.

However, unless and until both agree to amend the proposal, partners should stick to the plan. If either gives him or herself permission to set aside the agreement in favor of another course of action, trust is broken. For ongoing issues, a follow-up using *Take It to the Cross* is a fine way to take stock of progress made and to propose your next step in taking new ground financially, sexually, spiritually, or relationally. Getting better at parenting or managing a household, for instance, are endeavors requiring regular inspection and course correction to optimize outcomes. We can never get too good at living in line with our values and intentions.

What I Need From You

We have seen how conflict prompts defensiveness in all of us and how being vulnerable in unsafe situations can feel impossible. But after we make our proposal, it is good to follow up with a humble plea for **What I Need**.

If the proposal requires a change in our own attitude and behavior, we may wish to voice our need for patience from our mate. We may acknowledge our need for understanding or affection. We might realize we need their forgiveness or compassion. Whatever the need, expressing it vulnerably gives your partner the upper hand. Your mate can use the information to bless you and offer what you need, or use it to hurt you by withholding or doing the opposite of your heart's plea.

When He hung, naked and dying, surrounded by enemies, Jesus voiced his need from the cross—"I thirst!" Someone nearby took compassion and responded. Tragically, though, the pain-numbing agent he was offered was mixed with wine. Just the evening before, at His last meal with closest friends, Jesus had promised not to drink wine until he could drink with them in

His Father's kingdom. Being true to Himself and his commitment to those dear friends, Jesus refused the drink. As He experienced, saying "what I need" can lead to the additional pain of disappointment, but it opens the possibility for our need to be heard and satisfied.

Sometimes sharing our need underscores the centrality of relationship. No matter what topic of discussion, **What I Need** brings it back home to our longing for connection. Eros, or romantic love, is based on need, Getting back to what we really need from one another reminds us of why we got together in the first place. Attention, acceptance, affirmation, and affection are things we need on an ongoing basis. Security, romance, excitement, playfulness, adventure, warmth, commitment, companionship, stimulating conversation, challenge, and strength are all things we need from one another as well. We all need a partner who needs us. Love flourishes when we voice our needs and take turns serving one another.

Sharing your need deals a deathblow to self-protection and defensiveness. Once again, being vulnerable in the face of conflict is the key to connecting. Of course, vulnerability is the last thing our survival instincts would allow. But when we die to those survival urges, we come alive to the promptings of the Spirit. Dying to self radically demonstrates that saving our relationship is a higher priority than guarding the self.

Jesus went to the cross out of obedience to God, believing God would use it to restore relationship. We can learn to trust and obey our Father like Jesus did, and humbly revealing **What I Need** along with **What I Propose** is another way to make the process more personal and more powerful.

TAKE IT TO THE CROSS

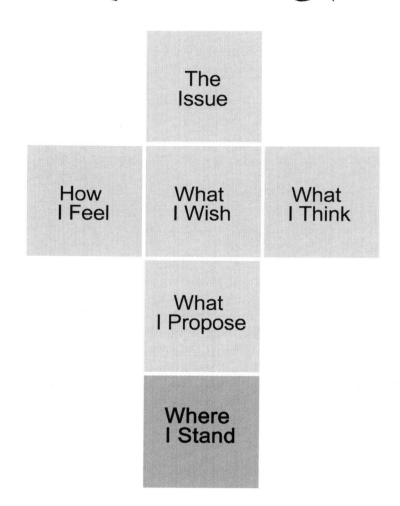

The Issue

How I Feel

What I Wish

What I Think

What I Propose

Where I Stand

CHAPTER 9

DECLARE YOUR COMMITMENT TO KEEP THE RELATIONSHIP CENTRAL

For some, the final step of the process is the easiest. We may struggle to define the issue, to put words to wishes, feelings, and fears, to clearly state what we think and believe along with a good proposal. But saying where we stand is simply a reminder of what is deepest in us. This may be voicing a commitment to children or to God, our commitment to honesty and integrity, or declaring our decision to stay the course and keep investing in the marriage. It can also include a statement of love and caring.

For others, reasserting a commitment to the marriage can feel impossible. Especially with repeated betrayal and deception, standing for the marriage can feel foolish. Even when dealing with a painful issue or disregard by a spouse, re-affirming commitment can take all we have. At times, it may not even make sense to be all in with a partner who only does the minimum. The power of the *Cross* allows us to die to our need to fix it and to guard our hearts from rejection. Especially if the marriage is on the rocks, we may only be able to say, "I want to stand for the marriage, but right now I can only stand on my commitment to be honest and courteous as we work through this together." In some cases, a divorce may have already occurred, and the *Cross* is being used to make decisions regarding scheduling or parenting the children.

Once again, it is important to address every step in the process. Physically walking the *Cross* gradually brings us closer to the one sitting at its foot. This last station brings us face to face with the one listening and with our deep values and unwavering commitments.

So after the speaker has stated the issue and expressed their wish, explored feelings and thoughts, and offered ideas and a tentative proposal, the focus moves to commitment. This will often be a sentence or two that reassures our partner of our love and loyalty. It provides opportunity to clarify what is crucial. **Where I Stand** is the place to relate our commitment and intention toward our partner, the relationship, and God.

The statement may be as brief as, "I love you, and I am committed to our marriage." It may also reference faith. "I know that God brought us together, and He will see us through." It may also put the issue in a bigger perspective. "This issue is huge for me, but regardless of what we decide, I stand committed to you and our relationship." Or "I am so happy we can work things out. In the grand scheme of things, my issue is probably not a big deal. By comparison, my love and commitment to you is huge."

Grounding the conversation with a brief statement of commitment is a powerful addition in the process. After having shared needs, thoughts, feelings and ideas, this final stop asks us to return to the foundation of our marriage and our faith. What is our commitment and where do we stand? These expressions of loyalty go a long way in calming our spouse and providing a context for our discussion.

In some ways, our commitments create a container for all the chaos and confusion that can be generated by conflict. They frame our interactions and make it safe for us to engage authentically and vulnerably. Saying **Where I Stand** forces me to look at the big picture and reminds me of the eternal perspective. When we look at our problems from the long-term vantage point, those problems shrink in size. They seem easier to tackle.

Plus, taking time to state our ultimate values prevents love being eclipsed by momentary desire or self-will. By taking our stand and stating our values, we decrease the likelihood that the strain and stress of current situations will move us away from our purpose and commitment.

Taking our stand at the foot of the *Cross*, eternal perspectives overshadow immediate frustrations. We come back to what brought us together in the first place, and remember that for us as Christians, the cross changes everything. It is God's means of reconciling with us and bringing us to peace with Him.

It was at the cross of Calvary that God took His stand for you. He faced unspeakable pain there to reveal the depth of His love for the world. The cross proves His willingness to lose what is most precious in order to convey His love for us. And while Jesus suffered for our sake, He speaks a hard word by announcing, *"Whoever wants to be my disciple must deny themselves and take up their cross daily and follow me"* (Luke 9:23).

The cross is a place of pain and suffering. It stirs our grief and uncovers our shame. But the cross also flows with love, tenderness, warmth, forgiveness, and grace. It is the weakness and the power of God. Covered by the blood of Jesus, God sees us as worthy and righteous. Standing in that flow and receiving His view of us changes the way we see one another. Since we have been accepted and have received freely, we can afford to give freely and demonstrate full acceptance, even when it is undeserved. Because God sees us as righteous in Christ, we can view each other in the same positive way. It takes practice, but we can do it!

CHAPTER 10

VALIDATE YOUR PARTNER BY REFLECTING WHAT YOU'VE HEARD

After each partner takes a turn walking the *Cross*, the other stands and gives a brief summary of what they heard. As they do, they can stand still at the head of the *Cross* or move from one card to another, encapsulating what was said at each juncture. However, no personal commentary is added.

Meanwhile, the other partner is now seated attentively at the foot of the cross. If notes were taken, it is perfectly fine for the person standing to refer to them while reflecting back what the other communicated.

This is something that requires practice for optimal skill. We must learn to demonstrate that we have truly listened, and not fallen into the trap of being so focused on what we want to share that we miss out on active listening. As Proverbs 18:13 reveals, *"To answer before listening —that is folly and shame."*

Hearing a spouse reiterate our message has a calming effect, allowing us to see that they "get" us. It serves to clarify and condense what has been shared. If we do a good job, our mate feels validated and appreciated. Our hearts soften as we feel understood.

To reflect back what we have heard is very honoring. As we learn to do it well, we find that understanding can be more powerful than agreement. While there are some perspectives and priorities we will never hold in common, validating each other by accurate reflection provides a deep connection. Taking time to articulate the other's point of view before sharing our own is huge. It is a practical working out of St. Francis' prayer—"May I not seek so much to be understood as to understand . . . " And it is a tangible expression of that understanding.

To do a good job of reiterating what our partner has shared, we must practice listening carefully with or without taking notes. Knowing we will feed back what our spouse has said ups the ante and boosts our attention.

If we wish to offer a good synopsis of our partner's heart in the matter, we must internalize their view enough to reflect it back in our own words. Although using their exact wording is occasionally effective, it runs the risk of sounding like we are just parroting back what was said. Accurate reflection in our own words is more powerful, because it demonstrates that we have processed and taken the other's communication to heart.

The Enormous Power of Empathy

If there is one thing I provide that fosters healing in my counseling practice, it is empathy. Empathy is the ability to enter another's experience enough to demonstrate through words, posture, facial expression, and tone of voice that we "get them." It is not that we necessarily agree with them or put ourselves in their circumstance, but through empathy we tune in to their deeply personal response to life's poignant and powerful moments. We don't have to experience the exact thoughts, feelings, wishes, or fears as another to show compassion and respect by putting words to our understanding. Differences between us fade into the background as we offer empathy.

Adopting the posture, tone, facial expression, and word choice that mirrors another helps them feel seen and felt. Connection and compromise come easier with intimate knowledge and mutual consideration. And feeling seen and validated is extremely rewarding.

Assumptions often interfere with empathy. I have on many occasions assumed I knew someone's response to an event, only to find I was absolutely wrong. I have learned, for example, that if someone tells me they have lost a close family member, I don't automatically assume that they are upset. Sometimes the death is a relief.

A funny example of misguided empathy occurred at one of our couples' retreats. Before a Sunday morning meeting, I greeted a participant walking up to the retreat house as I arrived. "Did you sleep well?" I asked. "No. We didn't sleep much last night," the young man replied. Immediately I rejoined, "Oh, I am so sorry!" Without missing a beat, he grinned broadly. "Don't be!" he exclaimed. Evidently, he and his bride were inspired by the chocolate and massage oil in the gift basket we provided, as well as by the "sex talk" from the night before!

A lack of empathy between husband and wife, though, is not funny. It can be heart-rending to sit with a couple who are not interested in hearing one another's hearts. A lack of attunement spells death to compassion. Intimacy is impossible when we do not even attempt to listen deeply or to show through posture, words, tone, and facial expression that we understand and that we care.

Judgments and Assumptions

To listen accurately, we must deliberately set aside our own narrow-sighted reality and reactions. Our personal view will sabotage the process if we are not able to silence it long enough to give undivided attention to the other. We must squelch our inner voices in order to hear all our mate is sharing. Being seated, silent, and taking notes all assist in mastering this difficult skill. If we are committed to becoming an expert listener, God will help us.

At any given moment, any of us is capable of lapsing into negativity. If we are frustrated or angry, hurt or confused, when we are sad or grieving, when we feel rejected or neglected, or if we are lonely, agitated, anxious, or bored, our view of things darkens. We are less optimistic, less playful, less courteous, and less able to believe the best about others. When we are in that negative brain space, our view is likely skewed, sometimes profoundly.

If we learn, as this tool teaches, to share our dim view as feelings—rather than facts—we make it immensely easier for our mate to listen and not disqualify our outlook. The moment we make the mistake of asserting our truth as *THE TRUTH*, we move the conversation from loving to legal and nonnegotiable.

The letter of the law is deadly. Speaking from the heart gives life. *"For the letter kills, but the Spirit gives life"* (2 Corinthians 3:6).

Likewise, when we feel judged, we mount a defense. We get even more entrenched in our stance and we are tempted to argue it to the death. On the other hand, when we feel understood and believe our partner has attempted to connect by reflecting with their words what we have spoken, we relax.

When it is clear that they hear us and are willing to affirm us right where we are, we feel empowered to move on. I see this constantly in my practice. When my patients feel seen, they begin to heal. Ironically, when offered acceptance just as we are, we feel empowered to change. We can only begin where we are. Empathy encourages growth.

Validation Vs. Agreement

When my wife sees my heart and validates that she hears me my deep feelings, longing and needs, I relax and I soften. When she is fully open to me, I open up to her. By the same token, as I do a good job attending and responding to Teri, she feels safe and confident. All of us are prone to resist relinquishing our position until it is acknowledged and affirmed.

Unfortunately, when dealing with our mate, we fear that validating their point of view may make them believe we agree. We don't see how to acknowledge and affirm them without sacrificing our own reality. But courageous practice disciplines us in holding on to ourselves while holding out love and acceptance to our mate. Feeling empathy empowers us to shift and behave responsibly.

Affirming your mate's experience is different than saying he or she is right. We can be respectful and open without showing pity or being condescending. Validation communicates acknowledgement and demonstrates the respect and the understanding we are all need, even when our concerns are illogical or seem petty.

When reflecting, resist the urge to jump to conclusions based on your partner's sharing. For example, "You said you feel lonely when I watch sports on TV. You probably think I am lazy and don't care about you."

Do try to summarize the gist of your partner's declarations in your own words, but remain true to the core message. Imagine my wife and me addressing the issue of time together. "Sometimes," she says, "I feel abandoned and lonely when you work late." If I reflect, "You hate it when I work late, and you are desperate to be with someone," I am likely projecting my own interpretation. Doing so risks stimulating feelings of disconnection. When we add to or assign meanings and motives, we risk making our mate feel accused rather than reassured.

Resisting our partner's viewpoints actually strengthens them, because it encourages them to push back and try harder to make their point. Acceptance, though, makes it easier for them to shift. Validation signals that we received the messages they sent—we get their feelings, perceptions, thoughts, needs, and desires. It shows grace and promotes peace. And when we are at peace with our mate and with ourselves just as we are, we are able to shift and change.

Truth is like sunshine, but grace is what waters our marriage garden. Both of us are likely to flourish as we engage respectfully and lovingly. We need grace most when we feel broken or confused, and when we release our unguarded reactions to troubling situations. *"Gracious words are like a honeycomb, sweetness to the soul and health to the body"* (Proverbs 16:24, English Standard Version).

Go to Your Corners!

Naturally, all of this takes practice, and we will have lapses in our desire for harmony. To be frank, there are times I catch myself trying to pick a fight because I feel agitated and want an excuse to vent. In this case, I can get even angrier if Teri doesn't take the bait to fight.

When things do escalate, though, asking for a time-out can be a great help. Heated discussions often lead to hasty reactions and hurtful words. This is a cycle we must interrupt. Thus, if either partner senses things ramping up, propose a break and a time to meet again later. Taking time out does not come naturally to many of us, because we want resolution *now*. However, learning to put on the brakes in communication can avoid wreckage and regret.

A timeout can be a selfless act of respect for the partnership. Taking a break allows us to step back and ask,

- "What do I most need right now?"
- "How am I feeling about myself in this moment?"
- "Is there something going on in me or my life that needs attention?"
- "Is there something I need to share with my spouse that I am avoiding?"
- "Do I need to cut myself or my partner some slack?"
- "Is their behavior mirroring some character defect in me that I need to address?"
- "Why am I being triggered?"
- "What is at stake here?"

Honest self-examination and reflection can reveal the source of unconscious distancing. If we are afraid to talk about an issue or we are dealing with shame, we may find "reasons" to come home late or avoid intimate conversation. We may collude with one another to keep our lives so busy we don't have time to connect deeply. Sometimes the fear of rejection or neglect is so strong we don't want to go there.

Before I learned to ask for sex when I was in the mood, I was always trying to read the signs. Was she in the mood? Might I get lucky? I recall one night being confused as I crawled into bed. I had just broached a touchy subject as Teri and I stood in the bathroom going through our bedtime rituals. Why, I wondered, had I touched on something so volatile when earlier I clearly wanted to get naked with her? To my chagrin, further reflection showed me that I picked a fight because I felt uncertain of a warm reception to my bid for affection. Getting into an argument put the kibosh on my desire to be close. Animosity, it turns out, is a great antidote to the fear of rejection. "I don't even care if you don't want me. I don't want you either!"

When we avoid reaching for one another, we avoid the sting of rejection, but we will not feel the balm of connection either. Being open to one another's bids for attention takes desire and practice, but we can all get better at it. We grow in understanding and intimacy by learning to tune in to what our partner is saying and reflecting back what we see and hear.

It is admittedly painstaking and feels forced when we first attempt reflective listening. But skills get easier with practice. Our brains are good at creating pathways and will assist us in performing important and complex tasks. Like riding a bicycle, learning to listen well and reflect with empathy can be challenging at first. Once we get the hang of it, though, we can put our skill into practice whenever the need arises. But be aware, it will always require your conscious decision and concerted effort. You have to want to ride. And you must get on the bike!

CHAPTER 11

WHAT IF YOU ARE STUCK?

No doubt some reading this book are in extremely difficult marriages. While *Take It to the Cross* is an enormously helpful tool, some will refuse to pick it up. As my wife, Teri, warns, some are tempted to use a tool as a weapon. Some will want to use it to authorize brutal honesty or might try to use it as a way to manipulate or control. Some will take a condescending attitude or use sarcasm or interject scripture to promote guilt in their mate. Obviously, a tool is most effective when used as designed. Fortunately, the tool itself interrupts many unhealthy habits of interaction around challenging issues. Using it consistently will change us and our approach to almost any conversation.

Even if your mate flatly refuses to try this method of addressing problems, it does not prevent you exploring your own wishes, fears, feelings, and thoughts. You will discover that connecting with your underlying emotions brings greater clarity about your reactions and what triggers them. Even when your partner is stubbornly resistant, sharing your heart and mind along with a thoughtful proposal and expressed commitment, whether verbally or on paper, will undoubtedly allow you to feel better about your own communication, and it might just reach them as well.

In the parable of the sower, Jesus reveals that our task will not always yield the desired result. Three out of four seeds may not produce fruit. Yet, in the end, we are not responsible for changing our mate or for making things happen. We are, though, held accountable for the way we relate. Are we *"speaking the truth in love"* (Ephesians 4:15)? When we plant good seed, we can let it go. We do the work and ask God to do the miracle. Sometimes the miracle will be a change in our mate, but equally as powerful and miraculous can be a change in our attitude. Finding peace and joy in adverse circumstances is evidence of God in us.

> *Though the fig tree does not bud*
>> *and there are no grapes on the vines,*
> *though the olive crop fails*
>> *and the fields produce no food,*
> *though there are no sheep in the pen*
>> *and no cattle in the stalls,*
> *yet I will rejoice in the LORD,*
>> *I will be joyful in God my Savior.*
>
> *The Sovereign LORD is my strength;*
>> *he makes my feet like the feet of a deer,*
>> *he enables me to tread on the heights.*

- Habakkuk 3:17-19

Modify Your Approach to Maximize Impact

Differences in personality and style of relating present enormous challenges in problem solving. Even when two people want to arrive at the same place, they may instinctively choose different routes. When navigating through difficulties, don't get off course by insisting on your own way or your own time frame. Be willing to modify your approach based on knowing your partner. For example, some partners communicate directly, while others use an indirect style. A direct approach is, "I want to go out for sushi," in contrast to the indirect, "What do you think we should do for dinner?"

Sometimes using fewer or more words can radically affect the impact of a message on the hearer. In general, men need to use more words to order to connect well with their wives. Women, on the other hand, would often do better using fewer words with a husband or son. Setting aside what is normal for us can bless others and greatly enhance our chances of being heard.

Additionally, men often need time to process information and feelings. They don't tend to change direction quickly. Women, as a group, can alter course rapidly, like a sailboat adjusting for the prevailing winds. Men are more like barges. While barges are built for bearing weight, they sacrifice maneuverability. They do not respond to pressure to turn rapidly. However, a cable exerting slow, steady tension on one corner can turn the massive vessel with patient persistence. Pushing harder, making demands, or badgering a man will seldom produce the desired change without resentment. Sometimes we must wait on God to do His work. We can trust Him to use His influence for good. *In the Lord's hand the king's heart is a stream of water that he channels toward all who please him*–(Proverbs 21:1).

We must be sure to leave our requests active, like a seed in the soil. When either receives initial resistance, we may be tempted to give up. "I knew you wouldn't go for it." "Just forget I asked!" "I never get anywhere with you!" Like disconnecting the cable from the barge, these communications let our partner off the hook. In contrast, "I can see your point, but I would still like for you to consider it," or, "If you change your mind, you know where to find me," keep the invitation active and give our mate a chance to have a change of heart.

As sailboats, women respond best to a gentle breeze. In scripture, the word we translate "wind" is also the word for "breath" or "spirit." I like to think of our emotional and spiritual motivations like wind that can move us. Sharing tender feelings with a woman is likely to move her, while a man's more intense feelings can affect her like a blast, a strong gust of wind threatening to capsize her boat. A controlled breeze is powerful in moving a sailboat from one side of a lake to the other, where a tempest or storm can take her under. Sharing from his heart in a controlled way, a man's message more likely moves his mate. Marriage is not a business. We are in covenant, not under contract, and women in particular respond better to an emotional or spiritual appeal than to a legal precedent or defense.

Modifying our approach based on what we know of our mate can be tough, but it is a skill worth developing. When we extend ourselves to reach our mate by hearing well and validating their position, they will tend to turn and be more receptive to our way as well. Not only do we want to reach a destination, we want to feel good about how we got there.

Avoid Communication Killers

While there are many styles of relating that successful couples engage, there are several that are clearly damaging. Expressions of disdain, negative interpretations, escalation, stonewalling, and criticism always have a negative impact. Being aware of these destructive maneuvers and avoiding them fosters safety for an unhindered and vibrant marriage. For more on these destructive types of communication, read the works of John Gottman. I especially like *The Seven Principles for Making Marriage Work.* (Gottman, J. M., & Silver, N. (1999). The seven principles for making marriage work. New York: Crown.)

Processing on paper is another way to unpack the past and shed light on the current problem. A written letter can be far less threatening than a face-to-face encounter. Remember, whenever tensions rise or a conversation escalates, agree to take a "time-out" and cool down. This provides a perfect opportunity to write out your thoughts and feelings so you both come back with clarity and calmness.

Even if there is not a risk of volatility, it is tremendously helpful for each partner to process thoughts and feelings alone before meeting to *Take It to the Cross*. This prompts each to dig deep inside, working to uncover elements that impact the issue and our responses to it. As we excavate our hearts, we clear away much of the "dirt" of negative emotions prior to engaging together. The result can be powerful, allowing each to mine deep concerns and core needs. Bringing these to light exposes what is at stake and makes resolution faster and easier.

Don't Let Buts and Baggage Deter You

Some issues open old and deep wounds. When this happens, it may be necessary to enlist the aid of a pastor, counselor or coach, who can function as a "crossing guard" and help us cross over from conflict to peace. An independent view can provide immense help by leading the way to safety. We need outside help to be efficient and effective in navigating the challenges of life.

Simply having someone else in the room interrupts some of our bad habits. The presence of a third person makes us more conscious of how we interact verbally and non-verbally. A third person helps anchor us in reality and allows an outside interjection if communication becomes unproductive. A coach on the sidelines offers valuable feedback, challenging us to perform at our best and helping us avoid costly fouls. The best athletes and teams know the value of enlisting the aid of the best coach they can afford.

While I am a psychiatrist who specializes in relationships, it would be pride and foolishness for me to think all my knowledge and experience exempts me from needing to ask assistance. When my team is losing ground on the playing field of life, I need someone looking on from the sidelines. I can't fix what I can't see. The perspective of someone viewing the field fresh and from afar is invaluable. Don't think that just because you are a star quarterback you don't need to listen to a coach. Depriving yourself of a connection that can help you go from good to great is lamentable. If you balk at the idea of paying someone to enrich your marriage connection, the cost of doing it yourself is often a huge reduction in satisfaction and intimacy. Furthermore, if things go badly, divorce can be devastating, emotionally and financially.

Tough Stuff

Some issues revolve around addictions or betrayals. In walking the *Cross*, or in my adamant refusal to do so, it may be clear that I am stuck in pride, fear or self-serving. Certain behaviors can be extremely intractable. For those with eating disorders or long-standing issues with weight, for instance, any issue around food may be like walking through a minefield. Similarly, a person with a skewed view of sex may need outside help to discover healthy sexuality and to heal from trauma or out-of-bounds behaviors from the past. Money issues can also reveal strongholds regarding security or material possessions. Jesus says we cannot serve God and mammon, the god of money. If we get a rush from spending or find our peace of mind through a strong 401K or bank balance, money may occupy a place in our hearts that is in competition with trusting God. If our mood is tied to finances, we may be dealing with a motivator that takes us away from finding our source of peace and joy in Him.

If walking the *Cross* reveals a need for help with deep issues, a good counselor can assist in cleaning out old wounds so they can heal properly. They may also provide the opportunity to rewire our thinking about things like self-image, performance and trust. It is a tragedy if we persist with coping strategies from the past that rob us of freedom and joy in the present. It is surprising how quickly some deep issues are resolved when openly acknowledged and addressed.

If a spiritual issue presents itself, a pastor, mentor, or accountability partner may help. Support groups may also offer an avenue of encouragement, challenge, and growth. Thousands of people dealing with addictions have found lasting help working the twelve steps in a group or one-on-one with a sponsor. *CrossTies*, a workbook I have written based on the Beatitudes, is a tool many have found useful in promoting spiritual growth and freedom from compulsive behaviors and unhealthy relational patterns. The exercises in the study empower us to bring thoughts, attitudes, and behaviors into line with the character of Jesus, like railroad crossties aligning one rail with the other.

You Can't See What You Can't See

"I will lead the blind by ways they have not known, along unfamiliar paths I will guide them; I will turn the darkness into light before them and make the rough places smooth. These are the things I will do; I will

not forsake them" (Isaiah 42:16).

Often we are like mice in a maze. We can't see how to get to the cheese. If we take the lid off our maze, though, and allow someone else an unobstructed view inside, the outsider's distance from our circumstance gives him or her opportunity to see what we cannot. "Turn left, left, and then right" may be all the direction I need to reach a corridor with a straight run for the cheese. In my practice, I can seem brilliant when working with other couples, but when it comes to problems in my own marriage, I can be a dunce.

Every excellent athlete gets coaching, and all of us perform better when we know someone is checking our work. Standing on the sidelines gives a coach the ability to observe and speak into the game. I work with some couples who determined from the outset to foster excellence in their marriage, so they schedule routine visits with me. Even couples who come in for only a six-month checkup tell me that it makes a significant difference in how well they do in-between times. All of us can attest to the boost our performance receives by knowing someone is paying attention to how we do our job.

As believers, our daily decisions are influenced by the certainty that we will stand before God and give an account. In light of that, don't be afraid to let others examine your choices today. Better be exposed now in front of one or two others than wait for a day when everything is revealed before God and everyone else. Jesus challenges us to live in the light and to come out of hiding. *"For there is nothing hidden that will not be disclosed, and nothing concealed that will not be known or brought out into the open"* (Luke 8:17).

Later, in Luke 12:2-3 He repeats the admonition, *"There is nothing concealed that will not be disclosed, or hidden that will not be made known. What you have said in the dark will be heard in the daylight, and what you have whispered in the ear in the inner rooms will be proclaimed from the roofs."* Let's not wait for the end for our lives to be examined. Practice examinations do wonders in preparing us for the final! As we follow Christ, we inevitably become more transparent with our mate, others, and God. And if we understand grace, we have no fear.

While the Holy Spirit is our comfort and counsel and can get our attention about things, it is difficult even for God to force us to pay attention to what we cannot see. All of us have blind spots, yet we often resist the feedback of those who know us best, particularly our mates. Even when an enemy attacks us verbally, we can usually find a grain of truth in the barrage. A third party can expose our blind spots as a couple and help us take a closer look at attitudes and behaviors that are holding us back. Feedback from others can help us navigate through difficult passages in life or break unhealthy relational habits. A more objective view or a slightly different approach can give the information and the impetus we need to shift.

Sometimes it is enough just to hear the same message from another source. In both Old and New Testaments we are encouraged to take advantage of outside counsel— *every matter may be established by the testimony of two or three witnesses*" (Matthew 18:16). What my wife has told me for years hits me differently when I hear it from someone else. When husband and wife argue in isolation, they have no one to use as tiebreaker. If we don't let others influence our thinking, how audacious to expect our spouse or child to be readily influenced by us! We should not expect our view to be adopted when we have not sought godly counsel or submitted our own views to examination by others.

Jumping to conclusions based on one perspective—someone else's or my own —is often foolish. In my deep desire to please Teri, I have on occasion taken actions that, in retrospect, were not a wise course. We once bought a Nissan Sentra for me to drive based largely on her research and influence, without my really asking myself what I wanted. It seemed easier to go with the flow. Although it served the purpose well enough, I and the Sentra never really belonged together. At other times, though, I have been equally fervent pursuing things that seemed good to me without fully honoring Teri. The purchase of our Avalanche is an example of a decision I drove to completion that turned out to be a costly mistake.

Go for Help!

Accountability and course correction are not always easy. We men do not like to stop and ask directions. But setting pride aside and seeking help can be huge if we wish to reach our destination in a timely way. God orchestrates circumstances in the lives of all his children to require connection with others for success.

Health psychologist, Kelly McGonigal, asserts that when you are stressed, your body releases oxytocin. This is a connection hormone, so when we reach out to others under stress, it helps us forge strong bonds. Oxytocin also improves heart health, and the relationships we form build stress resiliency. We can choose to go it alone, but we will lose some important battles if we fight in isolation.

As noted before, there is a war waging against your soul and the soul of your marriage. Reach out for help—and don't wait until you are desperate! The enemy is the one telling us we should be able to deal with things without any assistance. As the father of lies, he manipulates us through our fears. If we fear appearing weak, being judged or rejected, we are apt to miss out on the strength and security of godly community. God made us for relationship, and there are problems we encounter that are too big to face alone. He wants us available to assist others when they need it, and He asks all of us to be humble enough to receive help as well. Of course, it is more fun to give than to receive, but receiving is what equips us to give!

A Note to Men

FEAR RESIGNATION JUDGMENT RESENTMENT
ANGER PRIDE SHAME

These are the enemies of healthy conflict and we all deal with one or more of them from time to time. If you are going to have half a chance to have healthy conversations about things that matter most, you must agree to put aside these things temporarily and walk the cross.

As you do, you enter the danger, refusing to allow these barriers to intimacy to deter you. As you set them aside and engage, they begin to lose their power. No matter how it works out, using this or any other tool is a win for your relationship as long as you remember that engaging new things is the only way to grow and that even a failed attempt represents progress as long you do not move into judgment and resignation. "We can't do this! You didn't even try! Nothing will ever help!"

In my experience, men tend to resist using the cross more than women. Because it asks for vulnerability and makes us feel childlike, we men tend to back away. We have been trained through experience not to show weakness because it has left us open for ridicule and rejection, and we fail to realize that being vulnerable is the only way to effectively engage the heart of our mate and find healthy resolution to conflict.

We men have heard it. "Don't be a wuss!" And when it comes to engaging sports or life, we want to be manly and tough. When it comes to physical challenges and challenges in the work place, we want to man up. On the playing field, in the boardroom and the bedroom we want to show strength. And being tough is one way to do it.

At the end of the day, though, looking good, being right, feeling safe or in control don't do it. We have to get our hearts in the game. It is the one who engages with heart that prevails.

We had coaches help us on the playing field and mentors and bosses for the boardroom. But when it comes to the bedroom, we are often on our own.

While many a man would take a bullet to the chest to protect his wife and children, opening his chest by sharing his heart may be much more difficult. Dying to our defenses is one of the most challenging things we will ever do. But Jesus is clear, we men are to love our wives and to lay our lives down in the process. If we choose self-protection, we choose isolation.

For whoever wants to save their life will lose it, but whoever loses their life for me will find it.   -Matthew 16:25

Shake It Up!

Old patterns of communication die hard, especially when we feel defensive. One couple I counseled persistently reacted with destructive escalation even when utilizing *Take It to the Cross.* After several abysmal attempts at home, I asked them to do something fresh to interrupt their usual communication dance. I suggested adding humor or trying an unexpected or novel approach to help break the old mold.

When they came back for a follow up visit, they were uncharacteristically jovial. Curious, I asked how they were doing. Both readily agreed that things were much better. "We did what you told us, Doc," the husband said. "We tried something new. And it worked. Like a charm!" "Oh, yeah?" I queried. "So what was it?" A huge grin spread across his face. "Well, we did *Take It to the Cross,* but first, we took off all our clothes!"

CHAPTER 12

BACK TO THE GARDEN THROUGH THE CROSS

Life was working well for Jesus before He came to this planet. It was natural for Him to be supernatural. But He and God had a problem. Humans weren't fully convinced of their love. We just weren't getting it. That's part of why God sent Jesus: to speak our language and put Himself in our shoes. Out of obedience to His Father, Jesus set aside what was normal and good in order to communicate a loving message. He expects us to do the same.

The apostle Paul challenges us: *"Therefore if you have any encouragement from being united with Christ, if any comfort from his love, if any common sharing in the Spirit, if any tenderness and compassion, then make my joy complete by being like-minded, having the same love, being one in spirit and of one mind. Do nothing out of selfish ambition or vain conceit. Rather, in humility value others above yourselves, not looking to your own interests but each of you to the interests of the others.*

"In your relationships with one another, have the same mindset as Christ Jesus:

Who, being in very nature God, did not consider equality with God something to be used to his own advantage; rather, he made himself nothing by taking the very nature of a servant, being made in human likeness. And being found in appearance as a man, he humbled himself by becoming obedient to death—even death on a cross!" (Philippians 2:1-8).

Compassion and the Cross

Before Jesus came, God seemed far off and unapproachable. Often, He was seen as angry and withholding. While there were exceptions, like David and Moses, most of God's children related to Him from a distance, approaching Him with fear and trembling. But Jesus came to show us the nearness of God. He powerfully revealed the tender side of the Almighty.

Jesus' birth let us see God as a baby, vulnerable and weak. In the years that followed, the earth saw its Creator as a young child, a teenager and a young man. After that, He was seen feeding multitudes, healing sick and hanging out with outcasts and sinners. His feet on our soil allowed us to see and love God as Son, Brother, and Friend.

The crowning glory of the incarnation, though, was the cross. At the cross, Jesus is exposed in the most shameful way. On the cross, God is displayed at His weakest and most vulnerable. In Jesus' betrayal, arrest, and mockery of a trial, we see God standing judged and condemned rather than sitting as Judge. Seeing Him beaten by soldiers, rejected by the crowds, and ridiculed by onlookers, we see God spurned and disdained rather than one whose rejection we fear. Stripped naked and nailed to a rough-hewn cross, God becomes sacrifice, rather than one who demands our blood offerings. And as we see thorns mashed into the brow that heaven worships, we are brought to tears— tears for God. Yes, if we allow it, the cross pierces us; it opens our hearts to God. The cross presents us a vision of God that inspires compassion for the One who loves us enough to hold nothing in reserve.

By giving His most precious Son, the cross reveals the depth of God's love; there is nothing He will not do to reach us. The God of heaven could hammer us with power and intimidation. He could coerce with punishment and reward to enforce His ways. But the God of heaven wins us over by appealing to our hearts. The cross is our avenue to God and His way to reach us. Our approach to our mate must not be power and intimidation, whining or manipulation. Like God, our appeal must come from the heart. Revealing the suffering we feel because of love will finally win the day.

On the cross, the Bridegroom cries out to His bride, "This is how much I care! Here is my naked body. Here is my blood and my sweat. Here are my heart and my hands, pierced through for you. See my feet; I will not back away. Even in agony, I choose to forgive. And when I am forsaken, I will not lose hope. You may not see me always before you, but you are always on my mind. I have a place for you, and I will come again!"

Trying something new like *Take It to the Cross* is a stretch. It may even be painful. But with Jesus before us, we can abandon what is rightfully ours to embrace a new way. Like Him, we may be called on to take pain we don't deserve, and to reject privilege and self-protection that are ours by right.

Jesus endured the cross. Let Him show you how. He is with you and He will reward your efforts on the Great Day even if they seem futile now. Are you afraid to look silly? Afraid to get it wrong? Or are you simply unwilling to step outside your comfort? Let nothing hold you back! With God's strength, you can do it!

Practice, Patience, and Prayer

Patience, practice, and prayer keep us on a path to peace. With them, we can be confident of crossing over from conflict to cooperation and connection. The apostle Paul encourages us in Ephesians 4:2 and 3, *"Be completely humble and gentle; be patient, bearing with one another in love. Make every effort to keep the unity of the Spirit through the bond of peace."*

As we journey together, love and faithfulness keep us growing. They foster tenderness and trust. Love supplies momentum for us to scale shining heights together, and faithfulness keeps us trekking through dismal valleys. Peace becomes a constant companion when Jesus is at home in our hearts. *"He himself is our peace"* (Ephesians 2:14).

As we follow Him daily, Jesus leads us to joy and fulfillment.

As He has promised, when we lose our lives, we find them. All along the journey, our ups and downs reveal more of self, spouse, and Savior, and we revel in this adventure toward complete oneness and intimacy. There are more peaks ahead!

Praying together strengthens the bonds of intimacy and yields great rewards. In a conversation for three, we can confess our failures and fears and give voice to our dreams and desires as we turn toward heaven. We may find ourselves able to say things to God in prayer with our partner listening, that we would hesitate to share directly. "Lord, make me be a better husband. Help me tune in to my wife's needs. Help me show her that she's the only woman for me and that she is first in my life. Make me the man who inspires her respect and who makes her feel safe and cherished. And please, Lord, help her know how amazing it feels when she initiates sex or puts her mouth where no one else is allowed!" ☺

As we trust God more, we pray with increasing openness and vulnerability. We can be silly or serious. We can approach our dear Father in weakness or in strength, when we are enthusiastic or hopeless. We are not afraid to approach Him just as we are. *"Let us then approach God's throne of grace with confidence, so that we may receive mercy and find grace to help us in our time of need"* (Hebrews 4:16).

We can cast our cares on Him and say anything. We can ask for anything, knowing He will only give what is good. We can especially ask for wisdom as we consider difficult decisions. *"If any of you lacks wisdom, you should ask God, who gives generously to all without finding fault, and it will be given to you"* (James 1:5).

As we yield to Him in everything, we find him bringing harmony in our homes and using us to be a calm presence in every circumstance. As our trust grows, we may pray with confidence the prayer of Saint Francis, "Lord, make me an instrument of your peace . . ."

Ultimately, the cross moves us beyond our families and friends into the world, following Him as peacemakers. *"You will go out in joy and be led forth in peace; the mountains and hills will burst into song before you, and all the trees of the field will clap their hands"* (Isaiah 55:12).

The Marriage Garden

God's desire for every couple is to have what He bestowed on Adam and Eve. Because He wanted them to enjoy complete safety and trust, He created a serene and beautiful space where they could be open and unguarded. In the words of Genesis 2:25, *"Adam and his wife were both naked, and they felt no shame."* They had no fear of rejection and felt such connection with one another that their differences were not threatening in the least.

That is what we all need and long for. We yearn for a partnership that allows us to bring our strengths and our weaknesses, knowing we will be embraced and affirmed however we show up.

In the romance phase, this kind of connection and openness feels natural, but it isn't long in any marriage until our defenses and old relational patterns kick in and we lose that easy vulnerability.

But if we are willing to dig in and get a little dirty, God will help us cultivate our own Garden of Eden. And as we do, we can engage authentically and playfully, mindful that we are on the same side, remembering that our partner is not the enemy. We can admire and depend on one another's strengths, while valuing our weaknesses as opportunities to give and receive love and support.

By sharing from the heart, the pain of being judged and misunderstood gives way to the pleasure of being seen and accepted just as we are. And even in moments we are not on the same page, we can hold on to separate truths. We bear in mind that a man and woman can share physical time and space, and yet live in two very different realities.

As we are learning from quantum physics, two divergent facts can exist simultaneously and both be true. In this paradoxical reality, we hold out an offer of engagement, knowing the power of loving action breaks through barriers of logic and reason. Authentic encounters foster understanding and acceptance, which in turn dismantle dark strongholds of fear and shame so we can bask in the warmth and shining light of genuine friendship and lovemaking.

We do well to recognize that we all have a "memory of Eden."

We are born with a desire to reclaim the unguarded spontaneity, the safety, tenderness, playfulness and passion of life together in our own special garden. Every healthy marriage garden has its unique look and feel. The flowers and fruit reflect the choices and preferences of the gardeners. The design, the degree of formality or wildness, the symmetry or lack thereof, the colors and fragrances all flow from the unique blend of him and her.

In our marriage garden, we plow, plant and prune. We water and weed, asking God to bless us with a lush return on our labor. Eden means pleasure and Eden is where we want to live. We are all a bunch of kids trying to get back home. An if we hold on to hope, we can readily get back up when we fall down and keep on moving toward our own shimmering garden experience.

Awake, north wind,
and come, south wind!
Blow on my garden,
that its fragrance may spread everywhere.
Let my beloved come into his garden
and taste its choice fruits.

I have come into my garden, my sister, my bride;
I have gathered my myrrh with my spice.
I have eaten my honeycomb and my honey;
I have drunk my wine and my milk.

Eat, friends, and drink;
drink your fill of love.

Song of Songs 4:16–5:1

Go to It!

As noted in the beginning, a sexual connection can be about the best thing ever or the most horrifying of traumas, depending on our readiness to engage. I won't promise that engaging conflict will ever be as fun as sex, but it need not feel like an assault. As I hope you have seen, doing difficult conversations well allows conflict to open doors of understanding, tenderness, forgiveness and healing.

Our touchiest conversations are those which cultivate the soil of our hearts and plant seeds of fruitfulness. With intention, we can nurture a garden-type relationship where we can be safe and at home with one another. As we work together, addressing our differences with grace, the revelations and strategies we share will move us toward an exciting future with powerful partnership possibilities.

Jesus' story did not end at the cross. Resurrection followed! He died on a barren hill; He rose in a lush garden. *Take It to the Cross* is not an end in itself. Rather, it is designed as a path to serve you in finding new life together as a couple. Jesus came to reclaim the garden. He came for you to have life to the full!

When we feel dry and detached or hopeless and desperate, when we feel we are dying on the vine, we best reach out and communicate. We must die to self-protection in order to attempt rescuing our relationship. I must be willing to put "we" before "me".

Like the cross of Jesus, *Take It to the Cross* promotes death to self, which is never fun. But the cross helps kill what keeps us from life with God and from reaching one another's hearts. As we become willing, God frees us to love and to connect. The cross changed human history, and it can change ours. Embracing the cross as God's powerful means of redemption and reconciliation changes us internally and eternally transforms all our relationships. My deep desire and hope is that this book and the tool it describes will draw you closer to Jesus, to the cross, and to those you love.

Take it to the cross!

PART 2

TAKE IT TO THE CROSS AND KEY MARITAL CONFLICTS

Although the examples used in the opening chapters deal with relatively small issues, *Take It to the Cross* works with the most challenging of problems. The scenarios shared here illustrate couples finding new pathways to peace by putting the cross to work on tougher or more complex or challenging situations.

Each example highlights a common source of marital distress, making it easier to see that all couples struggle and must learn to negotiate to optimize harmony and happiness. Just reading the dialogue of another couple with a similar issue helps us feel we are not alone in the struggle. Some of these couples may put words to the muddle of feelings and thoughts that you experience and help move you down the path toward clear communication and resolution.

In cases where one partner or the other is extremely resistant to utilizing the tool, simply reading these examples together can have enormous impact. Hearing husbands and wives with similar dynamics and problems make strides in their problem solving builds hope and helps initiate a new dialogue. You might even try reading them aloud with husbands and wives reading their respective roles. If you do, it will help to be playful and give it your best dramatic interpretation!

All these dialogues are derived from personal experience and from working with couples who have utilized the *Cross* in their relationships, but they are composites and do not represent any individual couple. In each case, new possibilities become apparent as partners share their hearts and bare their souls. While conflict is the stimulus, intimacy results whenever we *Take It to the Cross*!

THREE CASE STUDIES

Sarah and Andy: The Sniper Mother-in-Law

"I'm pretty sure she hates me!" Sarah moaned as she strapped three-year-old Emma into her car seat. Andy gritted his teeth and snapped the buckle on four-month-old Jordan's car carrier. He got in and started the car.

"Aren't you going to say anything?" Sarah slipped into her seat and slammed the door. "Don't you even care that your mother treats me like I'm an idiot?"

"Of course I care! What do you want me to do about it?" The tires squealed as he backed out of the drive.

"You could speak up for one thing! I know she says a lot of it when you're not around, but you heard what she said at dinner about some women feeling obliged to have an opinion about everything."

"She wasn't talking about you! She made that comment after you told her what your friend Joy said about the election."

"Really, Andrew? She was taking a shot at me! Joy is my friend and I agree with her!"

"Just let it go. You know how my mother is."

"That's just the point. I do know how your mother is! And she is constantly sniping at me when I am around her. I feel like I never want to see her again!"

"Well, that will solve the problem! So our kids will never get to know their grandparents!"

"At this point, that wouldn't hurt my feelings."

"Look! Can we talk about this later?"

Sarah turned her head and looked away. "That's typical! You try to shut me up and act like we'll talk later, but we never do!"

"That's because it never goes anywhere! We both agree my mom is nuts. What do you want?"

"I want you to support me!"

They sat in silence for a few moments. Then Sarah spoke up again. "I'm sorry. How about we try *Take It to the Cross*? If we can't get anywhere, we can talk to our therapist about it."

"Okay. When?"

"How about Saturday morning after we have our coffee? We can let Emma watch cartoons, and hopefully Jordan will take a nap."

"All right. I don't know if there is a solution, but we can try it."

In the days leading to Saturday, Sarah and Andy had time to consider the issue. It wasn't anything new. The bad feelings between Sarah and her mother-in-law began before she and Andy were even engaged. Sarah broke up with Andy for a time while they were dating, and it was obvious that Andy's mom resented her for it. Even when they reconciled, Sarah felt she could do nothing right in her mother-in-law's eyes, and it seemed to be getting worse.

Saturday morning, Andy got both of them a cup of coffee while Sarah put Jordan down for a nap. They decided to *Take It to the Cross* in their bedroom with the door open so they could hear if Emma needed them. Andy put the cards out on the floor and invited Sarah to go first.

"The issue is your mom and how she treats me. I just can't stand it!"

Sarah stepped to the center card and read, **What I Wish**. "Oh, gosh," she said, "what I wish is that your mother liked me. I wish we had a great relationship and that she believed I was the best thing that ever happened to you. Because, of course," she added with a smile, "we both know I am!"

Andy grinned too.

Sarah stepped over to the right. "Okay, *How I Feel* and *What I Fear* Ohhh . . . What I fear . . . I guess I fear that I will never be good enough for your mom and that I will simply have to avoid her. And, I guess I also fear you will never stand up for me with her. And that makes me very sad."

Sarah moved to *What I Think*. "Really, Andy, I don't think any woman would ever be good enough for your mom. She has you and your brother on a pedestal. His fiancée feels the same way I do. Even though they aren't even married yet, she feels like your mother takes a condescending tone with her. She loves your dad, but dreads spending time with your mom."

Andy started to interrupt and then caught himself.

"I know a lot of it is not personal, but I can't help feeling upset whenever it happens. She would probably do it with anyone you married. I just happen to be the lucky girl! I do want our kids to know their grandparents, but sometimes I don't even think it's worth it!"

Sarah stepped back over to the feelings card. "When your mom makes a snide comment and you say nothing, I feel completely betrayed. It feels like someone has just punched me, and you just sit there watching. If you don't speak up, it feels like you agree with her or at least condone it. Really, sometimes it feels like you care more about her feelings than mine. I know you want me to just blow it off, but I can't! When you act like it is not happening, I feel completely insignificant."

Once more stepping to *What I Think*, Sarah explained, "I know our kids are too young to see it now, but I don't want them thinking it is okay for anyone to be rude and critical, least of all a family member. I don't want them seeing you sit by and do nothing about your mom's behavior. I know your dad never challenges her. I get that. He has to live with her. But we don't. And at this point, I don't care if she throws a fit!"

Once more, Sarah's feelings moved her back to the other arm of the cross. "I am ashamed to say it, but sometimes I feel like I hate her." Tears welled up in her eyes. "I know you would never cheat on me, but it's almost like she is the 'other woman' in our marriage. I need you to choose me over her! I know you don't understand it, but I need to see you do it."

After a moment, she continued. "I remember how I felt when you told her you didn't want her to come to our wedding if she couldn't be happy for us. That meant so much to me! You have no idea how good that felt for me to hear. *And* she got a lot nicer for a while."

She stepped across to share some more thoughts "Andy, I know you think your mom will never change, and that there is no point in addressing it. But Mary loves bragging on her grandkids, and if she knows she can't see them unless she behaves herself, I'm pretty sure she will find a way to do better. I want to believe that she will see how much we love each other and grow to accept me, too."

"I think I have an idea." Sarah stepped to **What I Propose**. "At first, I was going to propose that I just stay away from your mom completely and let you take Emma and later Jordan when he gets a little older. Now, though, I really think I need you to stand up for me. Otherwise, she would probably like it if she could have you and the kids without me. And because I know you hate to talk to her, I propose you write a letter, like the one our counselor had me write my dad. Tell her how we feel and make it clear we will end the visit any time she acts up. I want her to know that you are not her little boy any more—that you belong to me and you support me no matter what.

"Where I stand..." she stepped to the final card. "I am committed to you and our family. I want to have the best possible relationship with your mom and I think it will actually be good for her to see that you can do what your dad has never really done. Just remember what you said to her when you told her we were getting married. I felt so loved!" Sarah leaned forward and kissed Andy on the forehead.

He stood up and said, "Thanks, babe."

"Your turn," she sat where Andy had been. "Don't forget to say what you heard."

"Oh, yeah," Andy scratched his head. "I should have taken notes!

"Hmmm . . . The issue is my mom, and you wish she would disappear!" Sarah gave a comical frown and Andy chuckled. "Okay, maybe I'm the one who wishes that! You wish she liked you and that we could all get along. Is that right?"

"Yes," Sarah nodded, "but I'm afraid I'll never be good enough and you won't ever stand up for me."

"Right! I was just going to say that! You are afraid you'll never be good enough and that I won't ever stand up for you. Now, some of your feelings are anger and sadness, and you think that I need to stand up to her. You think she can change if it's the only way she can see the kids. Hmmm, sometimes you feel I don't care about you and that I care more about my mother. And . . ." He looked up as if searching for something more.

"And I feel betrayed when you don't speak up because I keep thinking you'll have my back." Sarah said softly.

"Right again!" Andy held up his forefinger. "You feel betrayed if I don't speak up because you really want me to have your back. Oh, and you feel small and powerless when it happens.

"Let's see, your proposal was to shoot her. Oh, wait! That was going to be my proposal!" He grinned again. "Your proposal was for me to write a letter to her, telling her we won't come if she doesn't act right. Where you stand is desperately in love with me, provided I let my mom know that what we want is more important to me than what she wants. Right?"

"Not too shabby, especially for someone who learned early on to tune out the woman in his life! And remember, I am not your mom!"

"Yes, Mother," Andy said mischievously. "Now it is my turn! He stepped forward to *What I Wish.* "Hmmm . . . What I wish is that my mom would miraculously become rational and sane. I also wish she were a nicer person and she would treat you like you deserve.

"What I think is you are right about my mom believing no one is good enough for her sons. In her eyes we can do no wrong. If there is a problem she always looks for someone else to blame. She's always been that way.

"I also think she doesn't see what a great wife and mother you are. She says whatever she thinks without considering anyone else's feelings. I think I just learned to tune her out. Maybe that is part of why I don't react when she talks trash, because I don't even hear it.

"Feelings—" Andy stepped to the right arm of the cross. "Hmmm . . . I feel pissed when I think of the times my mom has hurt you, but I also feel frustrated that you let her get to you. I hate the feeling of always trying to keep the peace. And I guess you are right, I feel like she will never change. That's kind of sad." He looked down at the card. "I don't think I have a fear, except maybe that I will always feel in the middle between you two."

Andy brow knitted and he rubbed his fist under his chin. "Oh, wow! I just realized that when I ask you to blow off what she says, that's exactly what my dad taught me to do. I remember one time she went off on me about something I did that made her look bad, and my dad just sat there. Later, he came and told me not to worry about it. He said, 'You know how your mother is. She doesn't mean everything she says. You have to understand; it's just her way.'

"From that time on, I guess I stopped paying attention to what she said so she couldn't hurt me. But that's what makes you feel hurt and unsafe around her!

"Oh, I guess those are thoughts!" Andy stepped across to **What I Think.** "Sorry. Now what I propose," Andy said as he stepped to that card, "is that I stop making excuses for my mom and asking you to just blow it off. I think it would help me to write down what I need to say, but maybe I should simply talk to her. I don't know. That might be better. I'm not sure how to tell her what we want, but maybe you can help me with that. And I am willing to stop going over there if she doesn't do better. It's a hassle anyway, with all the baby stuff right now.

"**Where I Stand...**" He stepped closer to Sarah, "is directly in front of you!" Another grin flashed as he stared into her brown eyes. "I stand amazed at how much you put up with for me, and I want to do whatever it takes for you to know I do have your back. And your front! Especially your front!" They both smiled as Andy leaned over to kiss her. "I do love you. You know that, don't you?"

"Yeah," Sarah said, "except when your mom is involved!"

"Hey! Give me a break!"

"Okay. My turn again!" Sarah moved back to stand at the

head of the *Cross* as Andy sat down.

"Let's see, the issue is your mom, and you wish she would become sane and rational. However, you fear I will always put you in the middle."

"Wait!" Andy interrupted. "I did not say that you would put me in the middle, but that I would feel in the middle. There's a difference."

"You're right. Thanks. You said that you would feel in the middle. Let's see, your feelings were anger at your mom and frustration with me, and you think since you learned to tune her out, you wish I would too. You feel hopeless about her, but you are willing to try. And you think she does not see what a great wife and mother I am.

"In your proposal, you agree with the letter idea, but you think you might want to talk to her instead. You think you will need help being clear about what you ask of her. You are also willing to stop visiting if she doesn't change how she treats me.

"And you stand very close to me, wanting me to know you have my front, which you shall have when I see you have my back!" Sarah smiled. "How did I do?"

"Pretty good. Go again."

"The issue and what I want haven't changed. I do feel like you finally realize how important this issue is to me. That makes me feel happy. I also feel some relief knowing we are making a plan.

"I think," Sarah stepped left, "I finally understand why you always tried to get me to ignore what your mom said and did. You were trying to make me feel better because it works for you and your dad. But it always made me feel worse. Strange, isn't it?

"I think that I will feel safer with you when I know you will take up for me. I know we don't always see eye to eye, but I do want you to support me even when you don't agree. I need you to choose me, especially when it comes to your mom. I just don't think she wants to let go of you.

"Also, I propose we get our therapist to help with the letter. Maybe he will have some ideas for some healthy boundaries. He gave me really good feedback on the letter to Dad. I propose you and Emma go by yourselves to the picnic this weekend. I don't want to deal with your mom again until we get this settled.

"As before, I stand committed to you and the kids. I want us to have the best relationship possible with your family."

"Even if they are whacked?" Andy grinned.

"Even then." Sarah winked. "As long as we learn to whack back!"

Andy chuckled as he took his place at the head of the cross and summarized what he just heard. He agreed with Sarah's proposal and asked that she set up an appointment to work on the letter.

While big and longstanding issues may need some outside help, *Take It to the Cross* clarifies the issue and reveals what is at stake. By fostering clarity and honest communication, couples find even the most difficult conversations easier and more productive.

When we see each other's heart, we find a way to connect.

Jeremy and Meredith - Sex. How often? Who leads?

Before Jeremy and Meredith got married, they had been sexually intimate on a number of occasions. Even though it was not in keeping with their beliefs, they rationalized that they were committed to one another, and so it was not that bad. They began with heavy petting and progressed to oral sex before they finally went "all the way." They had sexual intercourse only after they were engaged, and Meredith was taking an oral contraceptive. Neither of them had been that intimate with anyone else, so they had no fear of sexually transmitted diseases. During their dating and engagement, they were sexually playful and provocative with one another. They both enjoyed the tension and the attention. Sex was extremely pleasurable for both, so they believed that they would be completely compatible in marriage.

Now, two years into the marriage, Jeremy was frustrated. Meredith seemed disinterested. After she had rejected his advances on a number of occasions, Jeremy pursued her less.

They still had sex three or four times a month, which was plenty for Meredith. She was willing to be there for Jeremy, but she didn't initiate sex nor was she always in the mood to have an orgasm. More frustrating to Jeremy, she certainly wasn't prone to offering oral sex as she had when they were dating. When he expressed frustration, she became defensive.

Jeremy suggested they take sex to the *Cross*.

"Sounds like something you'd do!" Meredith chuckled.

Jeremy was much more adventurous than she when it came to sex. He had been known to talk her into being sexual in various places away from home, particularly when they were dating. Although she was a bit hesitant, Meredith had seen the value of using *Take It to the Cross* to address touchy subjects, so they agreed Saturday morning would be a good time, right after morning coffee and a walk.

On Saturday, Jeremy made coffee and brought it to the bedroom. He crawled in bed and snuggled up next to her.

"Maybe we should skip the talk and just do it," Meredith suggested.

"Very tempting offer!" He sipped his coffee.

"Maybe our issue is already solved?"

"Anything's possible. I still want to 'do it' with *Take It to the Cross, though.*"

"Figures," Meredith said. "You go first. I'll just sit here in bed and try to enjoy my coffee."

"What about our walk?"

"Let's just do this really fast and maybe it will count as aerobic exercise."

Jeremy laughed and and laid the *Take It to the Cross* cards on the floor so the foot of the cross was at the foot of the bed. He took his place at the top .

"The issue is S-E-X. Sex. And you are sexy."

"That's another issue and up for debate," Meredith muttered under her breath.

"No talking when I have the floor. I have the power to say anything and you must be silent. I say you are sexy. Let the record stand."

She rolled her eyes and waved at him to continue.

"Okay. Now **What I Wish**. Hmmm . . . In my perfect world I would make love to my wife many times every day. She would want me so badly that she would jump my bones whenever I got home at night . . .I saw your eyes roll. This is my fantasy. Your time will come! Let's see. Where was I? Oh yes, my wife is jumping my bones, and she loves oral sex as much as I do."

Jeremy looked down to his left and stepped to **How I Feel**. "Ah, my feelings about sex! I'd have to say I feel pretty darn good. I feel grateful to be a man, and I feel happy that you are a woman and that God got us together. It feels awesome! What I fear is that you will feel pressured or disinterested in sex while I feel frustrated and rejected, and that I would begin to fantasize about having a partner who wants me."

He stepped to **What I think**, "I think we are really good for each other. I think you are amazing and are beautiful. I don't think you know how beautiful you are and how lucky I am to have you. That makes me feel— like I need to move back to how I feel."

Jeremy took a long step back to the right. "I feel sad when you don't seem to believe me when I tell you are beautiful. I feel cheated when you dress in the closet where I can't see you. In a way, I guess I feel sorry for you because of my strong sex drive. I feel like I am bothering you when I want sex. When you don't seem interested, I feel sorry for myself, and sometimes I just want to withdraw."

She bit her lip and nodded, rubbing her temples hard.

"I feel confused because you enjoyed sex so much before we got married. The way I remember it, we first did it because you were pushing for it. Oh, I guess that's a thought, not a feeling." He stepped to the left arm of the cross. "I think you love me, but I don't think you know how much I need to feel your body close to mine. When we don't have sex very often, I get tense and irritable and then you don't want to be close. I think if you enjoyed sex as much as I do, we would do it a lot more. I don't know how to change that."

Jeremy moved back to the center. "I guess I wish for your sake that I needed sex less, and I wish for me that you wanted it more. **What I Propose.** I propose we have sex at least twice a week and that you initiate sex once a week and that we both try to connect more affectionately like we did when we were dating. I need you!"

Meredith cradled her coffee cup and stared into it.

Jeremy moved to the foot of the cross. "**Where I stand** is committed to you and our relationship. I love you. I don't want anyone else. You are the best."

He grabbed his coffee mug, climbed back onto the bed, and gave Meredith a kiss on the cheek.

"Thanks," she said. "That wasn't as bad as I thought it was going to be."

"Silly girl. Your turn, now."

"Okay. Just let me take one more swallow of coffee to fortify me. Mmmm . . . Here I go. Don't anybody try and stop me. I'm going now. I mean it!"

Jeremy gave her a playful nudge, and she put her feet on the floor.

"I need a potty break," she said.

"Now you're stalling."

"But we don't have stalls in our bathroom."

"Just go! But come back soon or I'll send a 'search potty!'"

When she returned, Meredith stood at the head of the *Cross*. "The issue is sex, which you want all day, every day. You think it was better before we got married, and you feel frustrated that we don't do it more. You think you like it a lot more than me, and sometimes you feel sorry for me and sometimes you feel sorry for yourself. Your proposal is that we have sex twice a week and that I initiate once a week. Did I get it right?"

"Mostly. But I want to make sure you got that I said *at least* twice a week. I also really want you to know how beautiful you are and how much it blesses me to look at you when you are dressing or undressed and how much better I feel when we are making love often."

"Okay. Got it!" Meredith said.

"Got what?" asked Jeremy. "You have to restate it."

"Okay. You want to get together for sex at least twice a week, and you want me to know I am beautiful, and you like to look at me, and you feel better when we make love a lot. And you stand committed to me and think I am the best!"

"Now you've got it. Thanks!"

"S-E-X," Meredith stepped to **What I Wish**. "I have to agree that I wish for you that my sex drive was stronger. I wish for me that sex was not so important for you. I wish we were perfectly matched and that I could be everything you want me to be sexually."

He pressed the back of his hand to his mouth and nodded slightly.

"**How I feel**," she stepped right, "is sad that our love life isn't better. I am afraid I can never be enough for you. I feel guilty sometimes, but I also feel pressure from you. I think," she stepped to the other side, "you don't intend to pressure me, but that's how it feels. Sometimes I don't feel like I can say no, so I avoid coming to bed, or I just ignore your signals."

He grimaced and chewed his lip.

"I think maybe it would help if we planned for times to be together. A lot of nights, I just feel exhausted. When you make a move for sex, I end up feeling in a bind." She stepped right. "It's like I have to ignore my own feelings and needs or ignore yours. Either way I end up feeling bad. If I give in, I sometimes feel used. If I resist, I feel like I am not a good wife. I think it ends up making me relate to sex as a problem. I end up dreading it, especially if I feel you are expecting me to get all hot and heavy. Sometimes I'm just not there."

She sighed and looked around the room, hands laced behind her head, and moved to **What I propose.**

"What I propose,is that you be patient with me. I think your proposal is not unreasonable, but it still kind of scares me. I think it would help me if we had a real date night every week. If we go out Friday night for dinner, then I can initiate sex when we come home. If we are out late, I propose we have sex after you go for your Saturday morning run. During the week, I would like it if you call me during the day and let me know if you want to get together that night. That will help me be ready and we can both make an effort to get to bed earlier. If I have a bad day or have something going on, I want to be able to negotiate for another day. And I propose that we not have sex when I am on my period. I think it will help me if there is one week a month where there is no expectation or pressure.

"And," she stepped forward, "I stand committed to you and our love for each other. I want to reclaim the spark we had and I want to love you better."

"Thank you, baby," Jeremy stood and kissed her, pulling her in for a hug.

"Not so fast, 'baby'! Remember, you still have to reflect that you heard what I had to say."

"But we already agree!"

"I know, but the goal is understanding, not just resolution. Besides, I had to do it! It's your turn now."

Jeremy reiterated the gist of what Meredith had expressed. After getting her validation, he added that he felt very lucky to have such a lovely and loving wife. He also said he felt grateful that she was willing to talk to him about the issue since he knew it was tough for her. Moving again to **What I Propose**, Jeremy said again that he was in full agreement with her plan.

"Even though I don't think it needs to be a part of the formal proposal," Jeremy said, "I hope you won't be so shy about dressing in front of me. I will try to rein myself in and not pounce. For me as a guy, just being able to look at your beautiful body is like a drink of cold water."

He moved to **Where I Stand**. "I stand committed to you as my wife. I love you more than you know, and I want to do a better job of showing it."

Jeremy moved toward his wife, and Meredith reached for him. "I love you, Jeremy. I'm glad you're mine."

"I love you, too, sweetie." Jeremy snuggled up to his wife. "Oh, yeah, we didn't set a start date for our proposal. And we are supposed to write it down, sign and date it."

"Careful. You'll lose your opportunity," Meredith said.

"This is an opportunity?"

"Could be . . ."

Kristin and Neil - Money Woes

"What is this?" Neil walked from the garage into the kitchen, gesturing toward the new garments on the counter. "More clothes? Were you shopping again?"

"And how was *your* day, darling?" Kristin snapped.

"Bad and getting worse, now that you ask." Neil snorted. "I thought I told you we were running close this month!"

"Leave me alone!" Kristin scooped up the clothing from the counter and darted for the bedroom.

"You don't even care! I bust my butt for this family and I get precious little thanks. The least you can do is rein in your shopping addiction!"

Neil heard the slam of the bedroom door and the small click of the lock. "This is all I need," he thought. "After the day I've had!"

He got a Coke, popped the lid and went out to the back porch, feeling deceived and frustrated He had already talked to her about getting on a budget, but she resisted, insisting that she would watch her spending, but it seemed she had no concept of the burden he carried about the finances. Every month, the credit card bill revealed charges he knew nothing about and they would argue finances again.

Six months earlier, on the verge of separation, they had gone to a "One Flesh" marriage retreat when they were and there recommitted to God and to each other. For about two months, they were doing remarkably better, and then things gradually started slipping.

Neil was tempted to believe the improvements had been an illusion and a waste of time. "Maybe she really doesn't care about me and only wants what she wants when she wants it!"

Then again, maybe it was more complicated. He had been

153

upset before he pulled in the driveway. It was a rough day at work and he wanted to have a quiet evening at home since the kids were out. He even imagined he might get lucky with Kristin.

But, seeing the new clothes on the counter, something snapped. The resentment toward Kristen was back an all he could see was selfish behavior and impulsiveness.

He thought how much he sometimes just wanted to be on his own. *If it weren't for the kids.* This same thought had prompted him to find the marriage retreat back in September.

He remembered how stuck they were then. Their parenting styles were so different, and as the kids were getting older, he and Kristin needed some way to be unified in disciplining them. At least that aspect of their marriage had improved. *Take It to the Cross* had helped them resolve some of those differences. "Maybe it would help now," he thought.

He knew he shouldn't talk to Kristin while he was still angry, so he decided to go to the gym. With all the stress at work, Neil hadn't been going to the gym to work out. *Maybe,that's part of the problem."*

He went to the bedroom. The door was locked, so he knocked.

"Go away!" Kristin said. "I don't want to talk to you!"

"Let me in! I need to change so I can go work out."

"Only if you promise you'll go!"

"Yes. I'll go."

She came to the door and let him in, but she didn't look at him. He went into the bathroom to change.

"Kristin, the kids won't be home until after 8:30. Unless you have something fixed, I am going to drink a protein shake and go to the gym. When I get back, I want us to use *Take It to the Cross* to see if we can figure something out about our finances. I'm pretty much at my limit."

Kristin didn't reply.

Neil bit his tongue. "Well, think about it. I'll only be gone about forty-five minutes."

When he returned home he felt a little less agitated. He microwaved some leftovers and took them back to the bedroom. The door was shut, but not locked this time. He went in.

She was sitting in bed reading. He went to the bedside table and pulled out the laminated cards for *Take It to the Cross.* He read over the instructions and the ground rules while he ate.

He turned to Kristin. "You ready?"

"I don't want to do it," she said. "You always think you're right and make everything my fault. I'll take the clothes back, if that will make you happy!"

"You know that won't solve the problem, Kristin. Somehow we need to get on the same page."

"Okay, fine," Kristin said. "But I don't want to stand on the cards. I'll just sit here."

Neil made his appeal. "I think it will work better if we walk through it."

"You can if you want to." Kristin was still looking down at her book.

"Okay, but at least put your book down." Neil arranged the cards on the floor with the foot of the cross pointed toward Kristin's side of the bed.

Neil took one more bite and stood on **The Issue.** "Well, the issue is money and how we deal with it."

Kristen sniffed and rolled her eyes.

He stepped to the next card. "What I wish is that we didn't have to worry about money at all. I wish we were independently wealthy and neither of us had to work. I wish the kids' college was paid for and that we had a second home at the beach."

He smiled at her, but she did not seem to notice.

He stepped to **How I Feel.** "Although I'm not as angry as I was earlier, it makes me mad that we had an agreement and you disregarded it. I feel disrespected and ignored. When I look at the credit card bill and see purchases you never mentioned, I feel anxious and deceived. When I ask you and you get defensive, I get angry. Then you treat me like I am a bully."

"You are a bully!" She looked up from her book and glared.

"You can only say that when it's your turn. What I fear is that you will never be happy."

She rolled her eyes, but he tried to ignore it.

"What I think." Neil stepped to the other side of the *Cross,* "is that you never saw your parents work together as a team. It's like they simply try to stay out of each other's way. You view every discussion as a power struggle. You see me as controlling, but for me, it's a matter of cooperation and respect. When you spend money and we haven't talked about it, I feel kicked in the gut."

Kristen ducked her head back toward her book.

"I know your mother still hides things from your dad, but I don't want that. Sometimes I feel you treat me as if I were a tyrant, but I want to feel like partners. Now I see our children adopting an entitled attitude. When they want something, they believe they should have it." He stepped back over to the feeling card. "Honestly, sometimes I just want to run away and start over somewhere else. I do love you and the kids, but I don't feel like anyone appreciates how much I sacrifice for all of you. I feel like I always have to put the brakes on things."

He knotted his hands in his hair and grimaced.

"*What I Propose* is that we find out if the church is offering the 'Financial Peace University' course again. Don said it made a huge difference for him and Linda. That could help us get on a budget and maybe finally get out of debt." Neil read as he stepped to *Where I Stand*. "*Where I Stand*, is committed to doing a better job with our finances. I want us to be more generous in our giving. I don't want us to feel like we are pulling in opposite directions. I want all four of us to be grateful and responsible with money. I know you don't always believe it, Kristin, but I do love you."

"Fine," she said. "You can see when they offer the course again. I'll at least try it out."

"Wait a second! You haven't taken your turn."

"What's the point? I agreed with your proposal!"

"The point is I want to hear from you, too. I really don't think I know it all or that our financial problems are all your fault. I know I have made a lot of bad decisions that have hurt us financially. It's just that we need to figure out how to do things better. Please, Kristin."

"I am not going to stand up."

"Okay." He sat on a nearby chair and grabbed his plate. "First you recap what you heard me say, and then you go through the process, too."

"All right, the issue is money and you wish we had tons of it. But you are afraid I still wouldn't be happy. You feel unappreciated and it ticks you off when I buy things we haven't agreed on. You don't want me to hide things, but you get mad when I leave them out like I did today. You think it's all because of how I was raised and you think the kids and I feel entitled. You want to do the class at the church so you can put me on a budget. And you are committed to do better with money." Kristin sighed.

Neil tried not to sound frustrated. "Yes. And I want you to know that I love you and want us to feel we are on the same team."

"Got it." She folded her arms and sat against the pillow in the bed. She peered over at the cards on the floor and began. "I guess I wish we didn't have to worry about money either. But I want a new house, a cook and a maid, too!" A trace of a smile appeared, but quickly vanished.

"What I fear is that we will always struggle financially, and you will treat me like I don't have a brain. I am not your child!"

"You are unbelievable!"

"Look who's talking now! I knew this wouldn't work!" She picked up her book.

"I'm sorry." Neil pressed his fingertips to his temple. "Please do it. I'll keep my mouth shut."

Kristin grumbled under her breath. "Whatever. . . **How I Feel**: Right now I feel like you just want to be right about everything. I feel like I can't win with you. Even when I am doing my best to manage expenses, you always find something to gripe about. It makes me not even want to try! Plus, you look at my closet but forget about the garage full of power tools you don't even use. And your car cost way more than mine."

He winced and clamped his jaws shut.

"I think in your mind, I should run to you about every decision. You talk about being partners. I think you just want control! And I don't agree about the kids. They have a lot less than most of their friends. I do tell them no. And those clothes on the counter were from Ross. I got six items for less than $30! And that's the first time this month I have spent anything on myself!"

Neil looked a little sheepish. "I'm sorry."

"I propose that I get $800 cash from the ATM every month for food, my clothes, and miscellaneous expenses. I'll put gas on the credit card, and the kids can ask you when they need something out of the ordinary. And where I stand, or rather *sit*, is ready for something better. Obviously, both of us feel mistrusted and disrespected. I also want to feel like we are working together. And I want to get out of debt, too."

"Thanks, Kristin. That helps," Neil stood up. "My turn again. Okay, what I heard from you was you wish for wealth and a staff of servants, but you fear that we will always be playing catch up and that I will treat you like you have no brain."

She bit her lip and nodded hard, her eyes a little misty.

"You feel angry and hopeless about our situation and how I treat you, and think I am controlling. You also pointed out that I spend money on power tools and my car. You don't think the kids are spoiled, and you want me to recognize when you are trying. You feel like I don't give you any credit."

She looked away and dragged her palm across her cheek.

"Let's see . . . You propose a monthly amount of $800 for everything but gas and extra stuff the kids need. And you stand—or sit—ready for something better. Like me, you are tired of the way we do business, and you want to get out of debt, too. How did I do?"

"Fine." Kristin shrugged.

Neil bit his tongue. He knew complaining about her attitude would not help.

"All right then," he said, "The issue and my wish have not changed. I feel glad we are doing this and even feel a little bit of hope. I hate that you feel like I want to control you, and I think," he stepped left, "that your idea might really help us avoid the power struggle. If we go on a cash basis I wouldn't be surprised by charges on the card, and you could use the money however you wanted. If you had the cash, you could spend it, and you wouldn't have me looking over your shoulder. But, I propose that you get $200 each week from the ATM. If you get it once a month, I am afraid it would be too easy to spend it before the month is out. If you get it every week and run out, it will only be a few days before you get more. Plus, you would actually be getting a little more than $800, since most months are more than four weeks long.

"I agree about the gas, but I also think medical and dental should go on the card, too. And prescriptions. We need a record of all that for taxes. If you and the kids eat out, I propose it comes out of the $200. But if we all go out, we'll use the credit card. And, of course, any unusual expenses we can talk about together. But I still think 'Financial Peace University' would help us. And where I stand is committed and hopeful. Earlier, I was thinking about how great it was after 'One Flesh.' I just want to get back that feeling."

She wasn't looking at him, but her arms were no longer folded. "Do I have to say what I heard again?"

"I would like it." His tone was gentle.

"Okay. You feel better about the situation and think the cash idea might help. You propose $200 a week for expenses, not including gas, medical, or eating out as a family. And you are committed. You want us to feel like we did after the retreat. Right?"

"You got the high points."

"I accept your proposal. I guess the only thing I want to add is that I think sometimes that you believe you are the only one that works hard. Trust me, you aren't the only one who feels unappreciated!"

"You're right," Neil nodded. "I could do a lot better job expressing how much I appreciate you. I'll try to do better. Thanks for doing this. I know it is not your favorite thing, so it means a lot. Do you want to write down what we agreed on or shall I? The instructions say we should sign and date it, so we can refer back to it later."

"You, please," Kristin said. "I want to take a bath before the kids get home."

"No problem. I'll shower after you get done. Thanks, again. I really think this will help."

#

Obviously, Kristin and Neil have many issues. But making even a little progress with a vexing problem can go a long way toward restoring hope and trust. Though it was a rough start, persistence paid off. It wasn't perfect, but it doesn't have to be.

For more vignettes of couples and families using *Take It to the Cross* to address pressing concerns, go to takeittothecross.net

APPENDICES

APPENDIX 1

SUGGESTED TOPICS TO EXPLORE

Here is a list of suggested topics you can explore using *Take It to the Cross*. I recommend keeping your own list and adding to it as new issues arise. Some couples like having a special notebook where they keep their notes, their proposals and their ideas for future discussions.

SEX—initiating; frequency; dealing with intimacy when there is sexual addiction or a history of infidelity or abuse

FINANCES—college funding, prioritizing one-off expenses, family members' requests for financial help, saving for the future, getting out of debt, discretionary income

HOUSEHOLD CHORES—division of chores for husband and wife, enlisting children in doing chores

DISCIPLINE OF CHILDREN—style, methods, specific challenges with strong-willed or special needs children

USE OF ELECTRONICS—how much, how long, age appropriateness for devices

TELEVISION – appropriate content, how much time

QUIET TIME

SPIRITUAL GROWTH—praying together, Bible study groups, home groups

WORSHIP ATTENDANCE

EXERCISE—when, where, how?

HEALTHY EATING

DAY OF REST

DAILY SCHEDULES

STRATEGIES FOR STAYING CONNECTED

DATE NIGHT

FAMILY VACATIONS

ROMANTIC GETAWAYS

PERSONAL RETREAT

AUTOMOBILE PURCHASE AND/OR MAINTENANCE

HOUSING

SIMPLIFYING SCHEDULES

ORGANIZATION STRATEGIES

CAREER

FRIENDS—same-sex friends, opposite-sex friends

REACHING OUT TO NEIGHBORS

HOSPITALITY

USE OF FREE TIME

BALANCE OF POWER IN THE RELATIONSHIP

BOUNDARIES WITH FAMILY

IN-LAWS

TIME TOGETHER—fun times, deep conversations, strategic planning

BLENDED FAMILY DYNAMICS—parenting together, interactions with ex-spouses

DECISIONS ABOUT FAMILY PLANNING—planning for pregnancy, birth control, adoption

ADULT CHILDREN AT HOME—expectations, time frames, responsibilities

CAREER OPTIONS—moving, accepting promotions that will limit family time, travelling

APPENDIX 2

SEVEN CORE CONFLICTS: RESOLVING THE MOST COMMON DISAGREEMENTS IN MARRIAGE

Below is an excerpt taken from an excellent book by Tim and Joy Downs. I find it heightens my awareness of the differences between Teri and me. Knowing our core issues helps us recognize and make allowances for them.

~~~~~~~~~~

Seven common underlying issues are the root causes of most of the conflicts in married life: Security, Loyalty, Responsibility, Caring, Order, Openness, and Connection.

Security is the need to be safe, the desire to know that you and yours are first of all protected from harm. There are two chief components of Security: the desire for Protection and the desire for Provision. Protection in its most basic form is the instinct for survival, but it also includes the longing for safety, stability, and even comfort. Provision is the desire to make sure everyone has enough, a desire that makes it necessary to both collect and save.

165

Because Security looks to the future, it would rather save than spend; because Security wants to provide, it would rather collect than throw away; because Security wants to protect, it has an aversion to risk. If Security is not your natural priority, your Security-minded partner can seem like a killjoy. Why can't he lighten up? But if Security is your priority, then your risk-taking partner seems just plain irresponsible. After all, it's safety we're talking about here, and surely that comes before everything else. We often fail to recognize the Security issue because it comes to us in the form of a dozen smaller, seemingly unrelated arguments—disagreements about money, and irresponsibility, and overprotecting the kids. But underneath it all is the issue of Security.

Loyalty is the dream of a mate who is unreservedly committed to you and to the relationship. Loyalty has two essential elements: Faithfulness and Priority. Faithfulness means being able to count on someone regardless of the issue and regardless of the circumstances. Faithfulness is what we vow first and foremost on our wedding day. Priority is something else we vow on our wedding day. Priority is what we mean by the phrase "forsaking all others." It means to move someone new into first place in your life. In the case of marriage, it means to put someone in her rightful place. Each of us is born with an instinctive "me first" attitude. But in marriage, every husband and wife has to cultivate a "we first" mentality—and each needs to know that his or her partner shares that value. We all need to know that the marriage will come before the in-laws, the best friends, even the children. Each of us desires our spouse to be faithful in the most basic sense, but the dream of Loyalty goes much deeper. Unseen aspects of Faithfulness and Priority cause conflict in day-to-day married life. Arguments about the role of the in-laws, the priority of the children, a husband's wandering eyes, and the amount of time spent at work and home are common examples of Loyalty conflicts.

Responsibility begins with the word ought: We ought to do this; we ought to take care of that. In marriage, one partner often has a greater sense of duty to follow the dictates of laws, customs, fashions, and the expectations of others. There are two components of the value of Responsibility: Obligation and Expectation. Obligation is an internal sense of what is owed. Every culture has thousands of unwritten customs and mores—things we're told we ought to do, but each of us has a different sense of just how important it really is to comply. That inner sense of oughtness is what we call Obligation. Expectation is your idea of what other people require of you. What do the neighbors expect of me? What do others think I should do? Expectation asks the question, "What will people think?" All of us are governed by some internal sense of Obligation and Expectation, but we don't always agree on what the rules are or how important it is that we obey them. This difference in internal value systems is what creates the Responsibility conflict, which often begins over issues like the upkeep of the house, obeying traffic laws, and social or family obligations.

Caring literally means "feeling and exhibiting concern and empathy for others." It's a great source of encouragement when someone is willing to Care—and a common source of conflict when he is not. There are two components of Caring, and one flows from the other like a river from a stream. The stream is Awareness, and the river it produces is Initiative. Awareness is mental and emotional alertness, an attitude of attentiveness to your mate's feelings and concerns. Initiative is what flows naturally from Awareness. Initiative is the willingness to engage your mate about a problem once you've become aware of it. It's encouraging to know that your mate is at least conscious of your concern, but it means a lot more when he's willing to do something about it. Concerns about a lack of Caring are voiced far more often by women than men. Women complain that their husbands are not aware and they do not initiate—and this is the beginning of the Caring conflict. Caring conflicts underlie many common disagreements: the failure to notice your mate's appearance, a lack of initiative on behalf of the kids, an unwillingness to deal with the messiness of your mate's emotions, and a failure to voice appreciation. All these issues have their roots in the issue of Caring.

Order is the desire to have things organized, orderly, and predictable. Some people want things to go according to plan. They like to know where everything is, and they want to know what comes next. But others would rather take life as it comes. They prefer things spontaneous, unexpected, and unpredictable. As life becomes more complex, Order becomes a critical issue and a source of great frustration for married couples. There are two aspects of Order: the desire for Structure and the desire for Control. Structure is the dream of having a place for everything and everything in its place, but it's much more than that. The desire for Structure can extend not only to household organization, but also to time, work, hobbies, shopping, leisure, and even sex. The underlying conviction is that anything works better with a plan. Control is the desire to somehow keep a firm grip on the steering wheel of life. It's an uncertain world. How can you increase your chances of success? By maintaining Control. And what better way to maintain Control than through forethought, planning, and discipline? If things are in Order, they're under Control—at least the odds seem more in your favor. Order conflicts may begin about household organization, personal records, punctuality, or the way you spend your leisure time, but they ultimately reduce to the underlying desires for Structure and Control.

Openness has to do with your attitude toward people and your need for privacy. Do groups of people invigorate you, or are your batteries drained by social interaction? Where do you instinctively go when you need to recharge—do you seek the company of others, or do you search for some space of your own? Openness has two chief components: Sociability and Energy. Sociability is the desire to be with other people, an orientation that finds its greatest fulfillment through connection with others. Sociable personalities are traditionally referred to as extroverts, while their privacy-seeking counterparts are known as introverts. Energy is the question of what drains you, and, when those mental and emotional fuel cells are depleted, what recharges you once again. Extroverts tend to recharge in social gatherings; people are an energy source to them. But introverts tend to recharge alone; people are an energy drain to them.

There's nothing wrong with being an introvert or an extrovert. But extroverted husbands often marry introverted wives—and vice versa—and that's where the trouble begins. Openness conflicts can start over anything where people are concerned, like social functions, time spent together vs. time spent alone, the priority of friendships, and the use of leisure time.

Connection problems arise when couples have different styles of Communication and Decision Making. Your Communication style is the way you seek to interact. Your style of interaction can be a bigger source of conflict than the actual words you choose. Unfortunately, couples are often completely unaware of the way they instinctively seek to Connect. Three pairs of conflicting Communication styles are common between married couples: linear vs. circular, emotional vs. cognitive, and interactive vs. didactic. Your Decision-Making style is the way you choose between options. There are dozens of life-changing decisions that husbands and wives must make together, and great frustration can result when couples approach decisions along very different paths. Three pairs of conflicting Decision-Making styles are common to couples: decisive vs. tentative, intuitive vs. evidential, and final vs. open-ended. Connection conflicts can begin about any topic at all, but quickly shift from the content of the discussion to its style. The argument is no longer about what you're saying, but how you're saying it—or not saying it. A Connection conflict makes it difficult to hear what your mate is saying at all. Connection problems are sometimes the most serious of the Seven Conflicts, because they may underlie the other six. Until we resolve our differences in style, it may be impossible to resolve our differences in substance. To really understand the Seven Conflicts, you might want to get the book by Tim and Joy Downs and read about each of them in detail. And don't forget to do the Inventories at the end of each chapter—that will help you understand how each of the Seven Conflicts relates to your marriage.

Downs, Tim; Downs, Joy (2003-02-01). *The Seven Conflicts: Resolving the Most Common Disagreements in Marriage* (Kindle Locations 1816-1896). Moody Publishers. Kindle Edition. This book has been pared down and is now titled, *One of Us Must Be Crazy and I'm Pretty Sure It's You (Making Sense of the Differences That Divide Us)*; used with permission of Moody Publishers.

TAKE IT TO THE CROSS ONLINE RESOURCES

For additional materials please visit:
TakeItToTheCross.net

You can learn more about Dr. Looney and his art at
PaulLooneyMD.com

Find more relational resources at
helpforyou.us

ABOUT THE AUTHOR

Dr. Paul Looney is a psychiatrist, pastor and painter. With a name that fits his profession, the "Looney Doc" believes humor goes a long way toward thriving in adversity. Viewing trial and conflict as God's way of urging growth and transformation, Paul and his wife, Teri, love helping folks overcome challenges to find fresh possibilities for living and loving. A Texan by birth, Paul's earliest memories are of growing up in the Rockies, so he and Teri split their time between Texas and Colorado. They facilitate a couple's retreat called "One Flesh" through their ministry, Hidden Manna. For more information, got to hiddenmanna.org. They love being with their sons, daughters-in-law and grandchildren.

TAKE IT TO THE CROSS TEAR-OUT
PAGES

THE ISSUE

This is the time to clarify or restate the issue to be discussed.

WHAT I WISH

In a perfect world, this is what you would wish for yourself and the other.

HOW I FEEL

Don't ask if your feelings are right or wrong.
Just express them! Include WHAT I FEAR.

WHAT I THINK

Here you give a positive, objective view.
Also share WHAT I BELIEVE.

WHAT I PROPOSE

Offer your suggested plan of action.
Be specific and give a time frame.

WHERE I STAND

Share your commitment to
the relationship and to God.

EMOTIONS CHART

When conflict arises, heartfelt communication fosters change and connection. Use this list to help share *How I Feel.*

INTEREST/EXCITEMENT
Curious
Excited
Hopeful
Relieved

WARMTH / TENDERNESS
Loving
Caring
Compassionate
Concerned
Playful
Affectionate
Appreciative
Admiring

OPTIMISM / TRUST
Peaceful
Hopeful
Grateful
Content
Confident
Determined
Trusting

REGRET / REMORSE
Apologetic
Sorrowful
Repentant
Regretful

HURT / SADNESS
Hurt
Rejected
Betrayed
Sad
Discouraged
Hopeless

SHAME / SHUTDOWN
Guilty
Ashamed
Humiliated
Defensive
Withdrawn
Numb

FEAR / UNCERTAINTY
Anxious
Afraid
Worried
Timid
Confused
ShockedHorrified

ANGER / DISDAIN
Irritated
Frustrated
Angry
Furious
Disgusted
Bitter

Made in the USA
San Bernardino, CA
28 February 2017